CAMBRIDGE
UNIVERSITY PRESS

CAMBRIDGE
Primary Mathematics

Workbook 4

Mary Wood & Emma Low

CAMBRIDGE
UNIVERSITY PRESS

University Printing House, Cambridge CB2 8BS, United Kingdom

One Liberty Plaza, 20th Floor, New York, NY 10006, USA

477 Williamstown Road, Port Melbourne, VIC 3207, Australia

314–321, 3rd Floor, Plot 3, Splendor Forum, Jasola District Centre, New Delhi – 110025, India

103 Penang Road, #05–06/07, Visioncrest Commercial, Singapore 238467

Cambridge University Press is part of the University of Cambridge.

It furthers the University's mission by disseminating knowledge in the pursuit of education, learning and research at the highest international levels of excellence.

www.cambridge.org
Information on this title: www.cambridge.org/9781108760027

First published 2014

Second edition 2021

20 19 18 17 16 15 14 13 12 11 10 9 8 7 6

Printed in Malaysia by Vivar Printing

A catalogue record for this publication is available from the British Library

ISBN 978-1-108-76002-7 Paperback with Digital Access (1 Year)

Additional resources for this publication at www.cambridge.org/9781108760027

Contents

How to use this book

This workbook provides questions for you to practise what you have learned in class. There is a unit to match each unit in your Learner's Book. Each exercise is divided into three parts:

- **Focus:** these questions help you to master the basics

- **Practice:** these questions help you to become more confident in using what you have learned

- **Challenge:** these questions will make you think very hard.

Each exercise is divided into three parts. You might not need to work on all of them. Your teacher will tell you which parts to do.

You will also find these features:

Important words that you will use. ⟶

difference	linear sequence	negative number	non-linear sequence	rule
sequence	spatial pattern	square number	term	term-to-term rule

Step-by-step examples showing a way to solve a problem. ⟶

There are often many different ways to solve a problem.

Worked example 1 ▶

The numbers in this sequence increase by 30 each time.

10, 40, 70, . . .

The sequence continues in the same way.

Which number in the sequence is closest to 200?

List the terms in the sequence.

The next terms in the sequence are:

$10 \xrightarrow{+30} 40 \xrightarrow{+30} 70 \xrightarrow{+30} 100 \xrightarrow{+30} 130 \xrightarrow{+30} 160 \xrightarrow{+30} 190 \xrightarrow{+30} 220$

Work out which term is closest to 200.

Answer: 190 is closest to 200.

These questions will help you develop your skills of thinking and working mathematically. ⟶

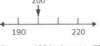 11 Write the missing number in this sequence.

1, 3, 6, 10, _____

Explain how you worked it out.

_____

_____

Thinking and Working Mathematically

There are some important skills that you will develop as you learn mathematics.

Specialising
is when I choose an example and check to see if it satisfies or does not satisfy specific mathematical criteria.

Characterising
is when I identify and describe the mathematical properties of an object.

Generalising
is when I recognise an underlying pattern by identifying many examples that satisfy the same mathematical criteria.

Classifying
is when I organise objects into groups according to their mathematical properties.

Critiquing
is when I compare and evaluate mathematical ideas, representations or solutions to identify advantages and disadvantages.

Improving
is when I refine mathematical ideas or representations to develop a more effective approach or solution.

Conjecturing
is when I form mathematical questions or ideas.

Convincing
is when I present evidence to justify or challenge a mathematical idea or solution.

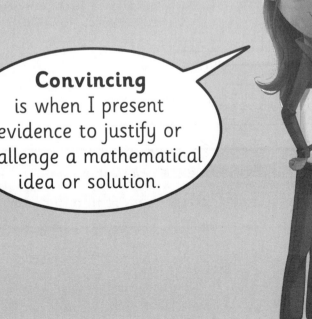

1 ▶ Numbers and the number system

❭ 1.1 Counting and sequences

Worked example 1

The numbers in this sequence increase by 30 each time.

10, 40, 70, . . .

The sequence continues in the same way.

Which number in the sequence is closest to 200?

List the terms in the sequence.

The next terms in the sequence are:

$$10 \xrightarrow{+30} 40 \xrightarrow{+30} 70 \xrightarrow{+30} 100 \xrightarrow{+30} 130 \xrightarrow{+30} 160 \xrightarrow{+30} 190 \xrightarrow{+30} 220$$

Work out which term is closest to 200.

Answer: 190 is closest to 200.

difference   linear sequence   negative number   non-linear sequence   rule
sequence   spatial pattern   square number   term   term-to-term rule

Exercise 1.1

Focus

1   Hassan shaded in grey these numbers on a hundred square.
The numbers form a pattern.

1	2	3	4	5	6	7	8	9	10
11	12	13	14	15	16	17	18	19	20
21	**22**	23	24	25	26	27	28	29	30
31	32	**33**	34	35	36	37	38	39	40
41	42	43	**44**	45	46	47	48	49	50
51	52	53	54	**55**	56	57	58	59	60
61	62	63	64	65	**66**	67	68	69	70
71	72	73	74	75	76	**77**	78	79	80
81	82	83	84	85	86	87	**88**	89	90
91	92	93	94	95	96	97	98	**99**	100

a   What is Hassan's rule for finding the next number?

_____

_____

b   What is the next number in his pattern?

_____

2   The sequence 10, 16, 22, . . . continues in the same way.
Write the next **two** numbers in the sequence.

_____ , _____

3 The rule for a sequence of numbers is 'add 3' each time.

$$1, 4, 7, 10, 13, \ldots$$

The sequence continues in the same way.
Circle the numbers that are **not** in the sequence.

22   28   33   40

4 A sequence has the first term 2020 and the term-to-term rule is 'add 11'.
Write the first five terms of the sequence.

_____ , _____ , _____ , _____ , _____

5 Write the next four terms in these linear sequences.

a 10, 7, 4, _____ , _____ , _____ , _____

b −9, −7, −5, _____ , _____ , _____ , _____

c 1095, 1060, 1025, _____ , _____ , _____ , _____

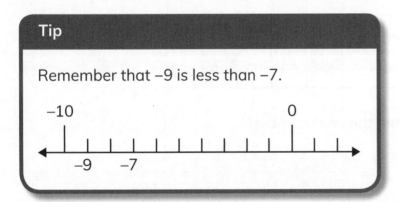

Tip

Remember that −9 is less than −7.

Practice

6 Here is part of a number sequence.
The numbers increase by 25 each time.

$$25, 50, 75, 100, 125, \ldots$$

Circle all the numbers below that will be in the sequence.

355   750   835   900   995

7   Amy makes a number sequence.
    The first term of her sequence is 1.
    Her term-to-term rule is 'add 7'.
    Amy says, 'If I keep adding 7, I will reach 77.'
    Is Amy correct? Explain your answer.

    _____

    _____

8   Here is part of a number sequence.
    The first number is missing.

    ⬜ $\xrightarrow{-5}$ 297 $\xrightarrow{-5}$ 292 $\xrightarrow{-5}$ 287

    Write the missing number.

    > **Tip**
    >
    > Remember to work backwards.

9   A sequence has first term 1001 and last term 1041.
    The term-to-term rule is 'add 5'.
    Write down **all** the terms in the sequence.

    _____

    _____

10 Each number in this sequence is double the previous number.
    Write the missing numbers.

    _____ , 3, 6, 12, 24, 48, _____

Challenge

11 Write the missing number in this sequence.

    1, 3, 6, 10, _____

    Explain how you worked it out.

    _____

    _____

12 The numbers in this sequence increase by 10 each time.

4, 14, 24, . . .

The sequence continues in the same way.
Write two numbers from the sequence that make a total of 68.

_____ and _____

> **Tip**
>
> You might find it useful to continue writing the terms of the sequence.

13 Describe each of the sequences below.

- Is the sequence linear or non-linear?

- What is the first term?

- What is the term-to-term rule?

- What are the next two terms in the sequence?

a 5, 9, 13, 17, . . .

_____

_____

_____

b 3, 11, 18, 24, . . .

_____

_____

_____

c 3, 6, 12, 24, . . .

_____

_____

_____

14 Write a sequence containing these numbers.
Your sequence must have at least one number between the two given numbers.
Describe the rule you use.
There could be different answers.

Tip

You could choose a linear or a non-linear sequence.

a   1 and 10

_____

_____

_____

b   6 and 20

_____

_____

_____

c   3 and 15

_____

_____

_____

d   1 and 100

_____

_____

_____

> 1.2 More on negative numbers

temperature   zero

Worked example 2

Here is a temperature scale.

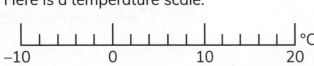

The temperature is 1° **below** freezing on a cold day.
Mark the position of this temperature on the scale with an arrow.

Each division on the number line represents 2 units.

1° below freezing is −1° and it is half way between −2 and 0.

Answer:

Exercise 1.2

Focus

1   Here is a thermometer. The arrow is pointing to 10 °C.

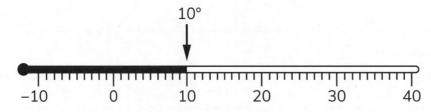

Draw an arrow on the thermometer pointing to −5 °C.

2 Here are some temperatures.

$$4\,°C \qquad -3\,°C \qquad 5\,°C \qquad 0\,°C \qquad -2\,°C$$

a Which is the warmest temperature? _____

b Which is the coldest temperature? _____

3 Look at the number line.

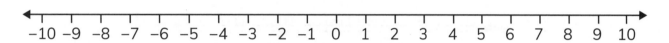

Write where you would land on the number line after these moves.

start	count on	end		start	count back	end
a (−4)	(1)	_____	**b** (6)	(6)	_____

start	count on	end		start	count back	end
c (−5)	(3)	_____	**d** (0)	(9)	_____

4 Circle the **larger** number in each pair.
Find the difference between the two numbers.
Use the number line to help you.

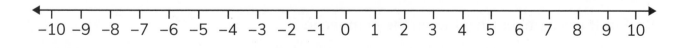

a −6   −2   Difference: _____

b −3   −1   Difference: _____

c 4   −4   Difference: _____

Practice

5 Here is part of a number line.
Write the missing numbers in the boxes.

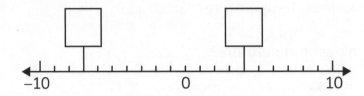

6 The thermometer shows a temperature of –8 °C.

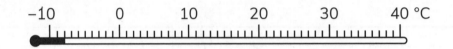

Draw arrows on the thermometer to point to these temperatures.

–4 °C   14 °C   –1 °C

7 Write the missing numbers in these sequences.

a   –12, –8, _____, 0, 4, 8, _____

b   –15, _____, –5, 0, 5, _____, _____

8 The temperature outside when Soraya arrived at school was –1 °C.
By lunchtime the temperature had risen by 8 °C.
What was the temperature at lunch time?

_____

Challenge

9 Put these numbers in order on the number line.

–1   1   –2   –3   –5

0

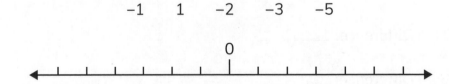

10 The temperature in Amsterdam is 2 °C.
The temperature in Helsinki is –7 °C.
How many degrees warmer is it in Amsterdam than in Helsinki?

_____

11 Here is a fridge freezer.

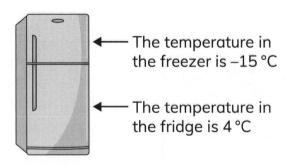

The temperature in the freezer is –15 °C

The temperature in the fridge is 4 °C

What is the difference in temperature between the fridge and the freezer?

_____

12 Here is part of a number line.
Write the missing numbers in the boxes.

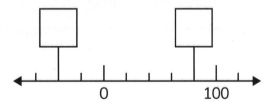

13 Mira counts on in threes starting at –13.
She says, 'If I start at –13 and keep adding 3, I will reach 0.'
Is Mira correct?
Explain your answer.

_____

_____

_____

> 1.3 Understanding place value

Worked example 3

Which number is 10 times smaller than seven thousand and seventy?

7700	707	7007	770	7070

1000s	100s	10s	1s
7	0	7	0
	7	0	7

When you divide by 10, all the digits move one place to the right.

Answer: 7070 ÷ 10 = 707

---

compose   decompose   equivalent   hundred thousand   million

place holder   regroup   ten thousand   thousand

Exercise 1.3

Focus

1   The distance from London in England to Budapest in Hungary is 1450 km.
Write the number 1450 in words.

_____

2   Circle the number that is five thousand and five.

50 005   5050   5005   50 050   5550

3   The table shows the number of visitors to a sports centre during four months.

Month	Number of visitors
January	6055
February	6505
March	6500
April	6550

Which month had the most visitors? _____

4   Complete this decomposition.

305 469 = [   ] + 5000 + [   ] + [   ] + 9

5   Heidi's password is a 5-digit number.

1   is in the ten thousands place

2   is in the ones place

3   is in the hundreds place

4   is in the thousands place

5   is in the tens place

What is Heidi's password?
Write your answer in words and in figures.

_____

_____

6 Fill in the missing numbers.

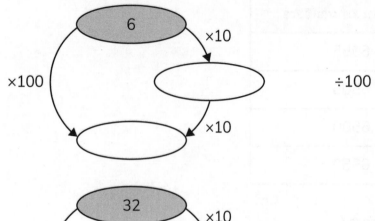

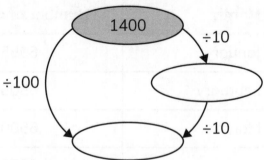

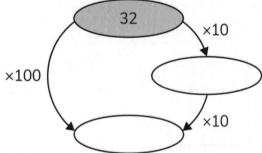

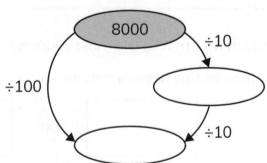

Practice

7 Tick the **largest** number that can be made using these four digit cards.

| 3 | 9 | 0 | 9 |

☐ Nine thousand nine hundred and three

☐ Nine thousand and thirty-nine

☐ Nine thousand nine hundred and thirty

☐ Nine thousand and ninety-three

8 Write in digits the number that is equivalent to 130 thousand + 3 tens.

_____

9 Here are four number cards.

A	eight hundred and fifty

B	five hundred and eight

C	five hundred and eighty

D	fifty eight

Write the letter of the card that is the answer to:

a 85×10 _____

b $5800 \div 10$ _____

c $5800 \div 100$ _____

d 58×10 _____

e $580 \div 10$ _____

f $50\,800 \div 100$ _____

10 Four students decompose the number 29 292.
Here are the results. One answer is incorrect.

A	$9000 + 90 + 20\,000 + 200 + 2$
B	$20\,000 + 9000 + 200 + 90 + 2$
C	$2 + 200 + 20\,000 + 90 + 9000$
D	$2 + 200 + 20\,000 + 90 + 900$

Which answer is incorrect? _____

Challenge

11 Write in words the **largest** number that can be made using all the digits
3, 1, 0, 9, 7 and 5.

_____

_____

12 Use the clues to solve the crossword.

Across

2. The digit in the ones place in the number 742 793.

5. Seven groups of ten.

6. The digit in the ten thousands place in 842 793.

Down

1. The name for 0, 1, 2, 3, 4, 5, 6, 7, 8 and 9.

3. The digit in the hundred thousands place in the number 814 682.

4. This digit is used to hold an empty place in a number.

13 Fill in the missing numbers.

a $358 \times 100 =$ ☐

b $3000 \div 100 =$ ☐

c $29 \times$ ☐ $= 2900$

d $2700 \div$ ☐ $= 27$

e ☐ $\div 100 = 3040$

14 Here are six number cards.

| 10 | 100 | 1000 | 35 | 305 | 350 |

Use two cards to complete each calculation. You can use a card more than once.

$$\boxed{} \div \boxed{} = 35$$

$$\boxed{} \times \boxed{} = 350$$

2 > Time and timetables

> 2.1 Time

Tick (✓) all the digital clocks that could show the same time as the analogue clock.

The analogue clock shows half past two, but it could be in the middle of the night or early afternoon.

Answer:

2:30 is a 12-hour digital time.

02:30 is a 24-hour digital time in the middle of the night.

14:30 is a 24-hour digital time in the afternoon.

You are **specialising** when you choose a digital time and check to see if it satisfies the criteria that it is the same time as the analogue clock.

a.m.   analogue clock   digital clock   hour   minute   p.m.   second

Exercise 2.1

Focus

1   Write the missing numbers.

    a   5 minutes = _____ seconds   b   4 hours = _____ minutes

    c   3 weeks = _____ days   d   _____ months = 2 years

    e   120 seconds = _____ minutes   f   600 minutes = _____ hours

2   Match each time to the correct digital clock.

    half past four   4 o'clock   half past three

    03:15   03:30   03:45   04:30   04:00

3   Find the time intervals for each pair of dates.

    a | 2 February 2020 | | 23 February 2020 | _____ weeks

    b | 1 January 2001 | | 31 December 2008 | _____ years

    c | 1 March 2009 | | 30 November 2010 | _____ months

4 Circle the digital time that shows the same time as this analogue clock.

3:15　　　　　3:45　　　　　9:15　　　　　9:45

5 Complete the following table using the information given.

Spoken time, 12-hour	Digital clock, 24-hour	Analogue clock
	08:50	
		afternoon
'eight thirty a.m.' or 'half past eight in the morning'		

6 Joe says, 'To change any time after midday from 12-hour to 24-hour time you just add 12 to the minutes.'
Is Joe correct?
Explain your answer.

_____

_____

Practice

7 Write the missing numbers.

a 2 years = _____ weeks
b 10 hours 30 minutes = _____ minutes

c _____ hours = 2 days 14 hours
d _____ months = 6 years

8 Complete the table to show the times shown by these clocks.
Use 12-hour clock time with a.m. or p.m.

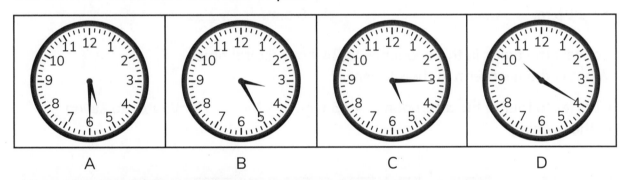

A   B   C   D

Clock letter	Time of day	12-hour clock time
A	evening	
B	night	
C	evening	
D	morning	

9 Match the times to the digital clocks.

Time	Digital clock

Time   **Digital clock**

quarter past 7 in the evening

twenty past ten in the morning

half past two in the afternoon

quarter to eleven in the morning

`10:20`

`07:15`

`14:30`

`19:15`

`02:30`

`10:45`

10 Write these times as 24-hour clock times.

a 10 a.m. _____   b 6 p.m. _____

c 11 p.m. _____   d 8 a.m. _____

11 Convert the times in this sequence to 24-hour digital times.
What is the next term in the sequence?

Quarter to four in the afternoon → 4.45 p.m. → 17:45 → 15 minutes to seven in the evening → ?

_____ → _____ → _____ → _____ → _____

Challenge

12 Complete the table to show the 24-hour digital clock times.

ten past four in the afternoon	
quarter past seven in the morning	
quarter to ten at night	

13 Write these times as 12-hour clock time with a.m. or p.m.

   a 15:10 _____   **b** 23:55 _____

   c 11:10 _____   **d** 03:05 _____

14 Pierre leaves home at the time shown on this analogue clock.

He arrives at school 20 minutes later.
Write the time he arrives at school in 24-hour digital time.

_____

15 Tick (✓) the time which is closest to 3 o'clock in the afternoon.

3.35 p.m. ☐   13:05 ☐   03:15 ☐   15:25 ☐   3.35 a.m. ☐

16 Five girls run a race.
Here are their times.

Sara	85 seconds
Milly	1 minute 34 seconds
Ingrid	91 seconds
Petra	1 minute 28 seconds
Neve	100 seconds

Place the girls in order at the end of the race.

_____	_____	_____	_____	_____
1st	2nd	3rd	4th	5th

> 2.2 Timetables and time intervals

Worked example 2

Here is part of a bus timetable.

Bergsig	12:00	14:16	14:30	16:16
Greenside	12:42	14:58	15:14	16:58
Newlands	13:22	15:35	16:00	17:36

calendar

leap year

time interval

timetable

Pablo catches the 3.14 p.m. bus at Greenside.

How long does it take him to travel to Newlands?

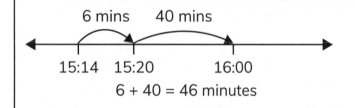

15:14   15:20   16:00

6 + 40 = 46 minutes

```
  60
-  14
-----
  46
-----
```

Use a time line. Work out the time from 15:14 to 15:20 and then from 15:20 to 16:00.

Or, subtract 14 minutes from 60 minutes (the number of minutes in an hour)

Answer: It takes him 46 minutes.

You are **critiquing** when you identify advantages and disadvantages of each method to help you choose the best method to use.

Exercise 2.2

Focus

1   Write how many minutes are between each pair of times.

a | 08:15 | | 08:40 | _____ minutes

b | 10:05 | | 10:55 | _____ minutes

c | 16:20 | | 16:55 | _____ minutes

2   Write the number of minutes between each of these times:

a

_____ minutes

b      Twenty-five past eight in the morning

_____ minutes

3   Here is a train timetable.

Train timetable			
	Train 1	Train 2	Train 3
Hightown	9.10 a.m.	10.05 a.m.	11.00 a.m.
Newbridge	9.25 a.m.	10.20 a.m.	11.15 a.m.
Bridgetown	9.50 a.m.	10.45 a.m.	11.40 a.m.
Donbury	10.00 a.m.	10.55 a.m.	11.50 a.m.

a   How long does it take to travel from Bridgetown to Donbury?   _____ minutes

b   How long would you have to wait for the next train if you

arrived at Hightown station at 10.30 a.m.?   _____ minutes

c   What time is the latest train you can catch at Newbridge to arrive

at Bridgetown by 11.20?   _____

Practice

4   Write how many minutes are between each pair of times.

   a | 11:05 | | 11:20 | _____ minutes

   b | 13:08 | | 13:28 | _____ minutes

   c | 14:08 | | 14:40 | _____ minutes

5   a   Bashir hires a bike. He must return it by 4 p.m.
       It is 3.25 p.m. now.
       How many minutes does he have left?

       _____ minutes

    b   Vijay hires a bike for 45 minutes.
       He takes the bike out at 3.10 p.m.
       At what time must he return the bike?

       _____

6   Alana wants to travel from Paris to London by train.
    She wants to arrive in London by 5.30 p.m.

Paris (depart)	12:13	13:13	14:43	15:13	16:13
London (arrive)	14:30	15:39	17:02	17:39	18:39

    What is the latest time she can leave Paris?

    _____

7   Here is the morning timetable for Ollie's class.

Time	Monday	Tuesday	Wednesday	Thursday	Friday
9.00–10.30	English	Maths	English	Maths	English
10.30–11.00	Break	Break	Break	Break	Break
11.00–12.00	Maths	Science	Maths	Science	Maths

    What is the total number of hours spent doing Science in one week?

    _____

Challenge

8   Tara takes 25 minutes to walk from home to school.
    She arrives at school at 9.00 a.m. What time did Tara leave home?

    _____

9   This clock has been reflected in a mirror.

   a   What time does the clock show? _____

   b   Bruno looks at the clock as he sets off walking to meet Leroy.

       He meets Leroy at 1.00 p.m. How long was Bruno walking? _____

10 Heidi goes swimming every Saturday.
    She goes swimming on Saturday, 1 December.
    Altogether, how many times does Heidi go swimming in December? _____

11 All buses from the bus station to the railway station take the same amount of time.
    Fill in the empty boxes to complete the timetable.

Bus timetable				
Bus station	8.02 a.m.	9.05 a.m.	10.01 a.m.	11.03 a.m.
Shopping centre	8.12 a.m.	9.15 a.m.	10.11 a.m.	
Park	8.36 a.m.	9.39 a.m.		
Railway station	8.54 a.m.	9.57 a.m.		

3 > Addition and subtraction of whole numbers

> 3.1 Using a symbol to represent a missing number or operation

> symbol

Worked example 1

Write the missing number.

85 + ☐ = 200

Always check whether the box represents only one digit or a complete number.

You need to find the difference between 85 and 200.

Method 1: Count on from 85.

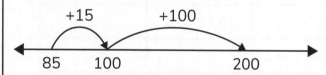

Method 2: Subtract 85 from 200.

200 – 85 = 115

Method 3: Use known facts.

85 + 15 = 100 so 85 + 115 = 200

Answer: 85 + 115 = 200

Exercise 3.1

Focus

1 Write the missing number.

37 + ☐ = 100

2 Write the missing number so that the scales balance.

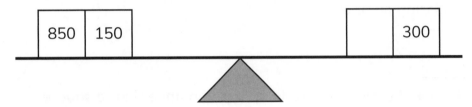

850 | 150   ☐ | 300

3 Write the missing digits.

4 ☐ + ☐ 4 = 100

4 Write the missing number.

☐ − 8 = 505

5 Here is a number square with two missing numbers.
   The numbers along each edge must add up to 80.
   Write the missing numbers.

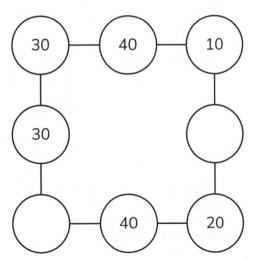

Practice

6 Write the missing number.

$\boxed{}$ + 7 + 8 = 28

7 Write the missing number.

$\boxed{}$ − 250 = 1000

8 Write the missing number.

48 − $\boxed{}$ = 26

9 The numbers in the two circles add up to the number in the square.

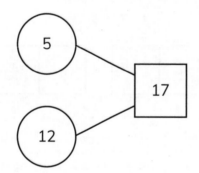

Use the same rule to find these missing numbers.

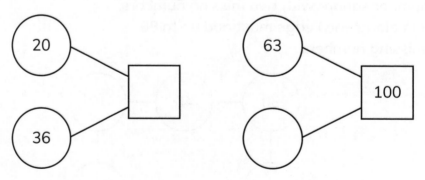

10 $\triangle$ and $\square$ are single digits

$\triangle + \square = 4$

Write all the possible answers for $\triangle$ and $\square$

11 Here are six digit cards.

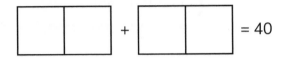

Use four of the cards to make this calculation correct.

☐☐ + ☐☐ = 40

Challenge

12 Complete the number sentence.

304 is _____ more than 296.

13 Break the 4-digit code to open the treasure chest.

65 – 58 = ☐ a

41 – 2 ☐ b = 12

86 – 79 = ☐ c

67 – ☐ d 8 = 39

Code is:

a	b	c	d

Tip

Write one digit in each lettered box.

14 Here is a number triangle with some numbers missing. The numbers along each edge must add up to 90. Use the numbers 30, 40, 50 and 60 to complete the number triangle.

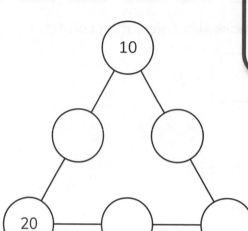

 15 Here are five number discs.

Use each number once so the total across is the same as the total down. Find different ways.

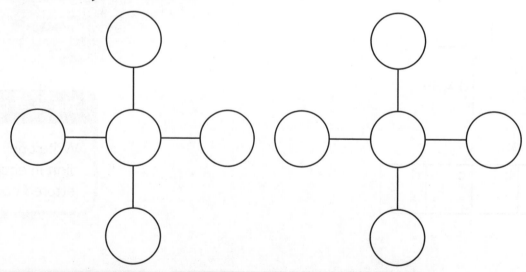

> 3.2 Addition and subtraction of whole numbers

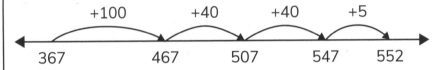

Worked example 2

Calculate 367 + 185.

Estimate:

367 is less than 400

185 is less than 200

So 367 + 185 is less than 600

| | | | | | | Use any method that you feel you can use quickly and efficiently. |

Calculate:

```
        +100        +40        +40        +5
   ┌────────────┐ ┌──────┐ ┌──────┐ ┌──────┐
◄──┴────────────▼─┴──────▼─┴──────▼─┴──────▼──►
  367          467       507      547      552
```

You can use jumps along a number line starting from the bigger number.

```
    3   6   7
+   1   8   5
  ───────────
    4   0   0     300 + 100
    1   4   0     60 + 80
        1   2     7 + 5
  ───────────
    5   5   2
```

Or you can set out the calculation vertically. Show as much working as you need.

Answer: 552

Worked example 3

Calculate 325 − 58.

Estimate:

325 is 330 to the nearest 10

58 is 60 to the nearest 10

330 − 60 = 270

Calculate:

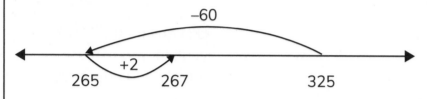

$$
\begin{array}{r}
325 \\
- \;\; 58 \\
\hline
267
\end{array}
$$

$$
\begin{array}{r}
200 + 110 + 15 \\
- \qquad\quad 50 + \;\; 8 \\
\hline
200 + \;\; 60 + \;\; 7
\end{array}
$$

Answer: 325 − 58 = 267

Use any method that you feel you can use quickly and efficiently.

You can 'count back' on a number line. You can count back 60 and forward 2 or count back 50 and then another 8.

Or you can set out the calculation vertically.

You will need to decompose the hundreds and tens in 325.

Show as much working as you need.

compose   decompose   difference   regroup

Exercise 3.2

Focus

1 Complete the addition questions.

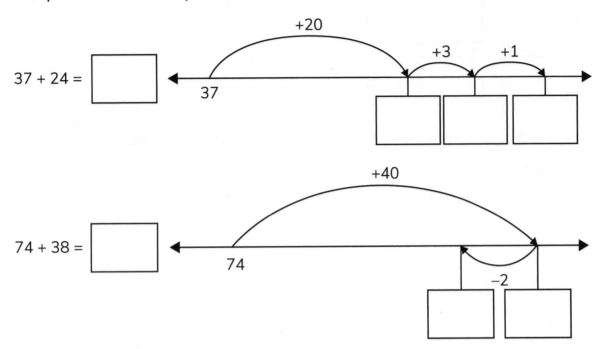

$37 + 24 =$ ☐

$74 + 38 =$ ☐

2 Complete the subtraction questions.

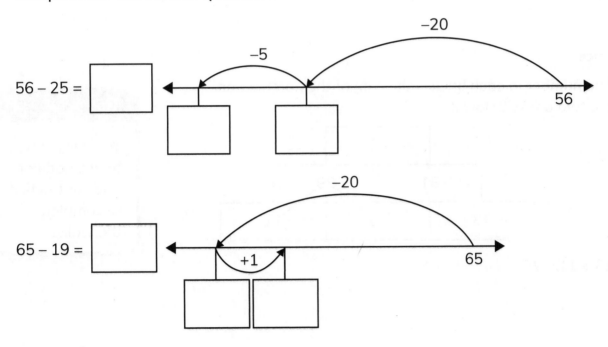

$56 - 25 =$ ☐

$65 - 19 =$ ☐

3 Complete the calculation 749 + 568.

749 = | 700 | + | | + | |

568 = | | + | | + | 8 |

| | + | | + | 17 | = | |

4 Use the most efficient method you can to complete these calculations.

   a   102 + 48

   b   154 − 140

Practice

5 The number in each brick is the sum of the numbers on the two bricks below it.

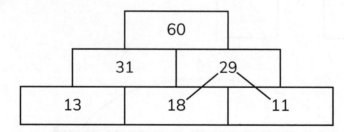

18 + 11 = 29

Tip

You will need to use addition and subtraction to complete the walls.

Complete these number walls.

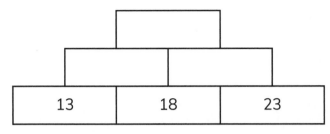

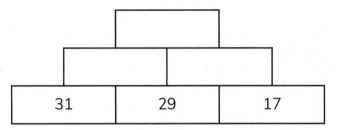

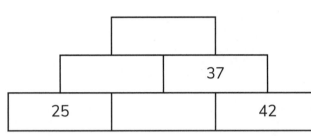

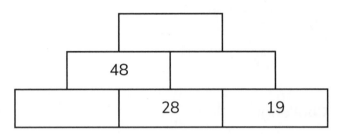

6   Complete the calculation 786 + 498.

	7	8	6
+	4	9	8
		1	4

Add the ones

7   Use the most efficient method you can to complete these calculations.

a   543 + 219   b   543 – 219

8 Calculate the difference between 983 and 389.

Challenge

9 Circle three numbers that total 750.

50   150   250   350   450

10 Here are four digit cards.

2 4 6 7

Use all four cards to make this calculation correct.

☐☐ + ☐☐ = 100

11 Circle the number that is closest to 900.

925   891   911   808   950

12 Write the missing digits to complete the calculations.

a

		1
−	3	4
2		

b

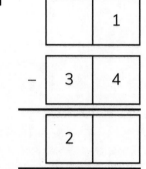

		1	5
−	1	5	
4			4

13 Naomi has six number cards.

She makes two 3-digit numbers and adds them together.

a What is the largest total Naomi can make?

_____

b What is the smallest total she can make?

_____

› 3.3 Generalising with odd and even numbers

Worked example 4

Is it always, sometimes or never true
that when you add two numbers
together you will get an even number?

1 + 2 = 3 which is odd	Test some examples by adding two numbers together.
2 + 4 = 6 which is even	Try to write a general statement.

Answer: It is sometimes true because when you add two numbers together the answer may be odd or even.

You are **generalising** when you look to find a rule.

counter-example   even   generalisation (general statement)   odd

Exercise 3.3

Focus

1   Shade all the odd numbers.
    What is the hidden letter?

416	636	50	32	412
232	861	220	657	154
198	423	8	53	654
110	5	851	825	730
404	53	676	595	358
206	45	294	687	590
682	566	742	174	552

2   Work out these calculations:

$5 + 11 =$ ☐ $23 + 19 =$ ☐ $101 + 5 =$ ☐

Each one is the sum of two odd numbers.
Use your answers to help you complete this general statement.

The sum of two odd numbers is always _____ .

3   Here are some statements about odd and even numbers.
    Join each calculation to the correct answer.

odd + odd =

even

odd + even =

odd

even + even =

4 Are the following statements sometimes, always or never true?
Explain each answer.

a The sum of two odd numbers is even.

_____

_____

b The sum of three odd numbers is even.

_____

_____

Practice

5 Work out these calculations:

$5 + 12 = \boxed{}$ $\qquad$ $23 + 20 = \boxed{}$ $\qquad$ $101 + 10 = \boxed{}$

Each one is the sum of one odd number and one even number.
Use your answers to help you complete this general statement.

The sum of one odd number and one even number is always _____ .

6 Here are some statements about odd and even numbers.
Tick(✓) the correct box next to each statement.

	True	Not true
odd + even = odd	☐	☐
odd + odd = even	☐	☐
odd − odd = odd	☐	☐

7 Leroy says, 'I add two odd numbers and one even number and my answer is 33.'
Explain why Leroy cannot be correct.

_____

_____

8 Mary says, 'The difference between two odd numbers is odd.'

Is this always true, sometimes true or never true? Explain your answer.

_____

_____

Challenge

9 Work out these calculations:

5 + 11 = ☐   22 + 19 = ☐   34 + 56 = ☐

213 + 35 = ☐   432 + 79 = ☐   876 + 432 = ☐

Use your answers to help you complete these general statements.

The sum of two odd numbers is always _____ .

The sum of two even numbers is always _____ .

The sum of one odd number and one even number is always _____ .

10 Here are some statements. Write **true** if the statement is correct.
Write **false** if it is not correct.

even + even = even _____   odd + odd = odd _____

even − even = even _____   odd − odd = odd _____

11 Here are four statements about odd and even numbers.
One statement is **wrong**. Put a cross (*X*) in the box by the **wrong** statement.

The sum of three even numbers is 24. ☐

The sum of three odd numbers is 22. ☐

The sum of two odd numbers is 20. ☐

The sum of two even numbers is 18. ☐

12 Is it always, sometimes or never true that the sum of four even numbers will divide exactly by 4?

_____

4 ➤ Probability

➤ 4.1 Likelihood

What is the likelihood of the spinner landing on grey? Use the language of chance.

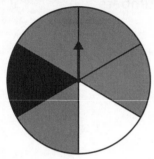

Step 1:

It is possible for the spinner to land on grey, so the likelihood cannot be described as 'no chance'.

Check if the outcome is impossible. An impossible outcome has 'no chance'.

Step 2:

The spinner could also land on black or white, so the likelihood cannot be described as 'certain'.

Check if the outcome is certain.

Step 3:

There are more outcomes that are grey than not grey, so it is likely the spinner will land on grey.

Are there more outcomes that are grey, or more outcomes that are not grey?

Answer: There is a good chance that the spinner will land on grey.

certain   even chance   good chance   likely   likelihood   maybe
no chance   outcome   poor chance

Exercise 4.1

Focus

1 Match the event to the description of its likelihood.
   The first one is done for you.

A die lands on an even number.   No chance

You will change into a fish tomorrow.   Poor chance

You will breathe today.   Even chance

You will turn left today.   Good chance

You will become famous tomorrow.   Certain

2 There are 3 balls in a bag: one white ball and two black balls.
   Write one of these colours in each space to make the sentences correct.

| red | white | black |

There is a good chance of taking a _____ ball from the bag.

There is a poor chance of taking a _____ ball from the bag.

It is impossible to take a _____ ball from the bag.

3   Ben used a website to simulate rolling a die 20 times. These are the outcomes.

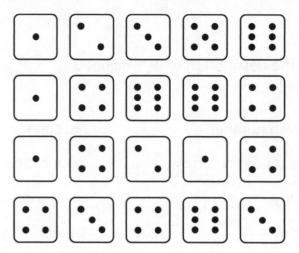

Use a website or a real die. Roll the die 10 times.
Draw the outcomes here.

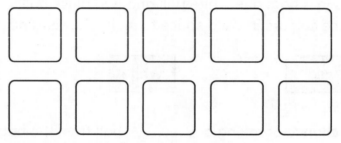

Complete this table to show the total rolls for you and Ben.

Number	Total
1	
2	
3	
4	
5	
6	

Complete the sentence:

There is no chance of rolling a number _____ .

Practice

4   Malik takes a sock without looking.
    Circle whether the sentences are
    true or false.

a   It is certain that the sock will be striped.   True / False

b   There is no chance of taking a plain sock.   True / False

c   There is a good chance of taking a sock that is not spotty.   True / False

d   There is a poor chance of taking a sock that is not checkered.   True / False

e   There is an even chance of taking a striped sock.   True / False

f   Maybe Malik will take a spotty sock.   True / False

Write a true sentence of your own about taking a sock without looking.
Use the language of chance.

_____

_____

5   Taking the ball with the star wins the game.
    Which bag has the greatest chance of winning?

A   B   C   D

6 Rose used an online random number generator to pick 20 numbers from 1 to 10.
These are the outcomes.

4	6	4	10	3	3	8	1	7	9
4	2	10	9	5	2	1	10	3	6

Use a random number generator to choose 10 more numbers.
(If you cannot use an online random number generator you could make
number cards 1 to 10 and pick one without looking 10 times.)

_____ _____ _____ _____ _____ _____ _____

_____ _____ _____

Complete the table to show the outcomes for you and Rose.

1	11	21
2	12	22
3	13	23
4	14	24
5	15	25
6	16	26
7	17	27
8	18	28
9	19	29
10	20	30

Complete the sentences.
Use words from the vocabulary box at the start of this unit to help you.

a   There is _____ _____ of getting 11.

b   It is certain to be a number less than _____ .

c   There is a _____ _____ of getting a 2.

Challenge

7 Malik takes a T-shirt from this rail without looking.
Write sentences using the language of chance about which colour T-shirt
will be taken from the rail.

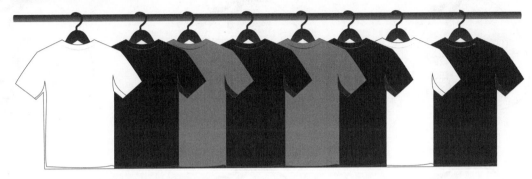

a Use **no chance** in your sentence.

_____

_____

b Use **certain** in your sentence.

_____

_____

c Use **poor chance** in your sentence.

_____

_____

d Use **likely** in your sentence.

_____

_____

e Use **even chance** in your sentence.

_____

_____

8 Taking the ball with the star wins the game.
   Put these bags in order from the greatest to the least chance of winning.

A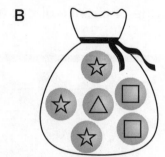

B

C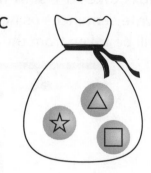

D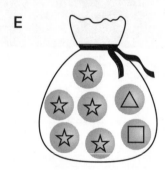

E

Greatest chance   Least chance

E   _____   _____   _____   A

9 Look at the words and phrases you have been using to describe likelihood
   in this Workbook and in your Learner's Book.
   Write the words and phrases you feel confident using in this box.

Write the words and phrases that you need to improve your use of in this box.

Draw some different-coloured balls in this bag.

Write sentences about the likelihood of taking different-coloured balls from the bag to practise using the words and phrases you need to improve.

_____

_____

_____

_____

_____

_____

Ask someone to check your use of the words and phrases.

5 ▷ Multiplication, multiples and factors

❯ 5.1 Tables, multiples and factors

Worked example 1

Write the missing factors of 20.

Factors of 20 = 1, ☐, ☐, ☐, ☐, 20

Here is a factor bug.

It is important to find **all** the factors of a number, so you need to be systematic.

You can write the factors of 20 on the factor bug's legs:

- Start with 1. $1 \times 20 = 20$
- Try 2. $2 \times 10 = 20$
- Try 3. $20 \div 3$ leaves a remainder so 3 is not a factor of 20
- Try 4. $4 \times 5 = 20$
- There are no more numbers to try as you have already included 5.

Answer: Factors of 20 = 1, 2, 4, 5, 10, 20

> **Tip**
>
> Instead of a factor bug you could draw different rectangles using 20 squares. The factors are the lengths and widths.

array   factor   inverse operations   multiple   product

Exercise 5.1

Focus

1 On the hundred square:

   - colour all the multiples of 2 in one colour

   - colour all the multiples of 5 in a different colour.

   - colour all the multiples of 7 in a different colour.

   What do you notice about the multiples of 10?

1	2	3	4	5	6	7	8	9	10
11	12	13	14	15	16	17	18	19	20
21	22	23	24	25	26	27	28	29	30
31	32	33	34	35	36	37	38	39	40
41	42	43	44	45	46	47	48	49	50
51	52	53	54	55	56	57	58	59	60
61	62	63	64	65	66	67	68	69	70
71	72	73	74	75	76	77	78	79	80
81	82	83	84	85	86	87	88	89	90
91	92	93	94	95	96	97	98	99	100

2 Write the missing numbers in this multiplication grid.

×	3		5
2	6	8	10
4	12	16	
	18		30

3 Complete this cross number puzzle.

1			2	3
	4		5	
6				7
8			9	

ACROSS
1. 6 × 8
2. 9 × 9
4. 24 ÷ 6
5. 63 ÷ 7
8. 10 × 6
9. 7 × 2

DOWN
1. 6 × 7
3. 3 × 6
6. 6 × 6
7. 8 × 3

4 The factor pairs of 8 are:

1 and 8

2 and 4

Write all the factor pairs of 18.

 1 and ▢

2 and

▢ and ▢

5 Complete the factor bugs for 36 and 45.

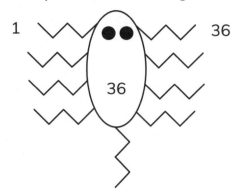

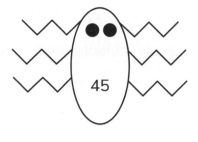

Practice

6 The number in each brick is the **product** of the two numbers below it.

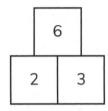

Write the missing numbers in these diagrams.

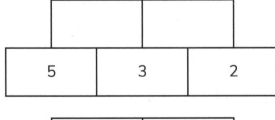

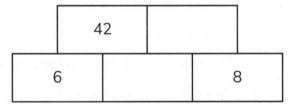

7 Use these signs:　　=　　<　　>

Write the correct sign in each box.

a　3 × 8 　☐　 5 × 5　　　　b　6 × 4 　☐　 4 × 6

c　7 × 8 　☐　 6 × 9　　　　d　4 × 4 　☐　 2 × 8

8 Circle all the numbers that are **not** multiples of 7.

7   17   27   37   47   57   67   77   87   97

9 Shade any multiples of 7 on this grid.

37	38	39
47	48	49
57	58	59

10 Here is a hexagon maze.

You need to go from the centre to one of the outside hexagons in two steps.

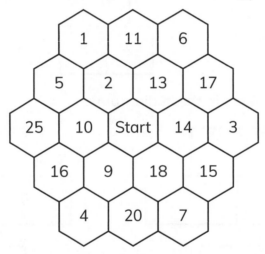

- Start in the centre.

- The next hexagon must be a multiple of 2.

- The next hexagon must be a multiple of 5.

What are all the possible paths you could take?

_____

11 Circle all the factors of 12.

1   2   3   4   6   8   12   24   36   72

Challenge

12 Complete these multiplication triangles.

The product of the two circles on each line is the number in the square.

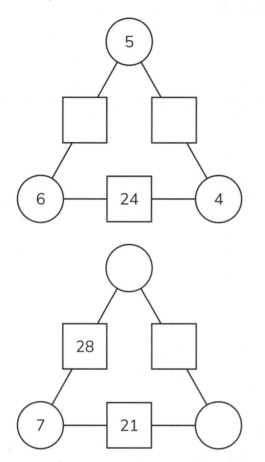
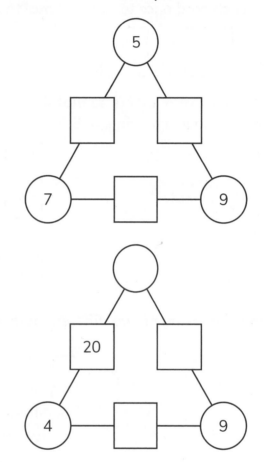

13 Complete the multiplication grids.

×	3	7	9	4	2
5					
					12
					6
					16
					8

×	3				10
	9				
		25			
			49		
6				36	
					100

14 Here are four digit cards.

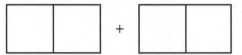

Use each card once to make a total that is a multiple of 7.

☐☐ + ☐☐

15 Cross out two numbers so that the sum of the remaining numbers in each row and column is a multiple of 5.

1	2	4	8
5	6	2	3
7	7	1	3
2	6	3	9

16 Saira is thinking of two different numbers.

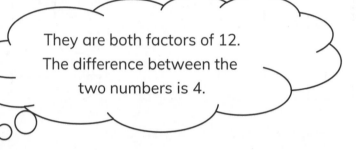

They are both factors of 12.
The difference between the
two numbers is 4.

What are Saira's numbers?

_____ _____

> 5.2 Multiplication

Worked example 2	
Calculate 345 × 9.	associative law carry

Estimate:

The answer will be less than 350 × 10 = 3500

Grid method:

×	300	40	5
9	2700	360	45

2700 + 360 + 45 = 3105

Answer: 3105

Estimate first by rounding 345 to 350 and 9 to 10.

Decompose 345 into hundreds, tens and ones.

Multiply 300 by 9, 40 by 9 and 5 by 9.

Add the products to give the answer.

Tip

You can use the same methods for multiplying 3-digit numbers by 1-digit numbers as you did for multiplying 2-digit numbers by 1-digit numbers.

Exercise 5.2

Focus

1   Complete this calculation.

$6 \times 15 = 6 \times 5 \times 3$

= ☐ × 3

= 90

2 The numbers in the circles are multiplied together to give the numbers in the squares between them. Fill in the missing numbers.

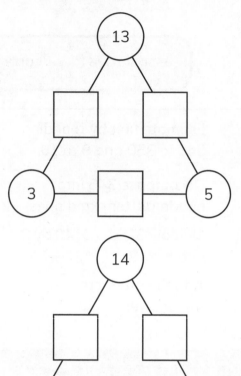

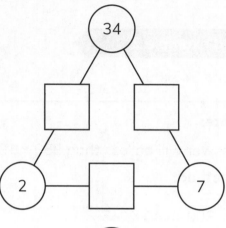

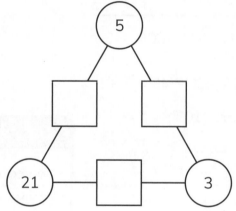

3 What is double 78?

_____

4 Find the product of 58 and 9.

_____

 5 Here are some number cards.

| 1 | 2 | 3 | 12 | 18 | 36 |

Use each card once to make three products with the **same** answer.

⬜ × ⬜ = ⬜   ⬜ × ⬜ = ⬜

⬜ × ⬜ = ⬜

Practice

6   **a**   Emma and Astrid calculate $9 \times 2 \times 5$.

Complete their calculations. Who chose the better method?

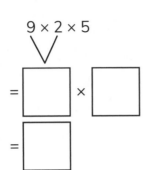

Emma's method

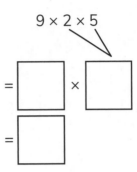

Astrid's method

_____

_____

b   Mario and Ian calculate $2 \times 5 \times 7$.

Complete their calculations. Who chose the better method?

Mario's method

Ian's method

_____

_____

7 Work out these calculations. Show your methods.
Remember to estimate first.

a 25×8　　　　**b** 69×6　　　　**c** 76×9

_____　　　　_____　　　　_____

8 Circle all the products equal to 2400.

900×3　　　　300×8　　　　600×4

300×7　　　　400×6　　　　800×3

9 Pierre uses the grid method to work out his calculations, but then spills
ink on his work. What numbers are under the ink blots?

$147 \times 3 =$

×	100	40	7
3	300	⬛	21

= ⬛

 10 Write what the missing digits could be.

| | | | × | | = 750

How many different answers can you find?

_____

_____

Challenge

11 Amy and Heidi work out 6×15.

Amy's method

Heidi's method

$6 \times 15 = 6 \times 5 \times 3$

$6 \times 15 = 3 \times 2 \times 15$

$= 30 \times 3$

$= 90$

$= 3 \times 30$

$= 90$

Which method do you like best?

Explain why.

Write two other methods for calculating 6×15.

_____

_____

12 Estimate the following first, then calculate. Show your working.

a 318×2 b 426×3 c 512×7

_____   _____   _____

13 Adah is thinking of a number. She divides the number by 3 and her answer is 234.

What number is Adah thinking of? _____

14 Write the **same** digit in each box to make the calculation correct.

3		6

$$\times \boxed{}$$

3	5	6	4

 15 Use the digits 3, 6, 7 and 8 to make the largest product.

			×		=	

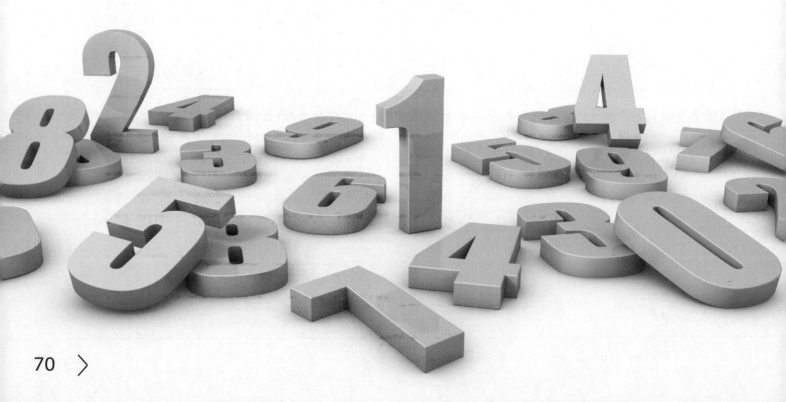

6 > 2D shapes

> 6.1 2D shapes and tessellation

Worked example 1

Tessellate this shape.

The shape has 6 sides and 6 vertices.
It is a hexagon.

Make a template of the shape by tracing it onto card.

Draw around the template.

Move the template so that the edge lines up with the shape you have already drawn.

Draw around the template.

Continue until you have filled the space with the tessellating shape.

The hexagon tessellates on its own without any gaps.

2D shape   parallel   polygon   regular   tessellation

Exercise 6.1

Focus

1   Find your way through the polygon maze. Only travel through squares marked with a polygon. Only travel vertically or horizontally between squares. You could use the polygon checklist to help you find the polygons.

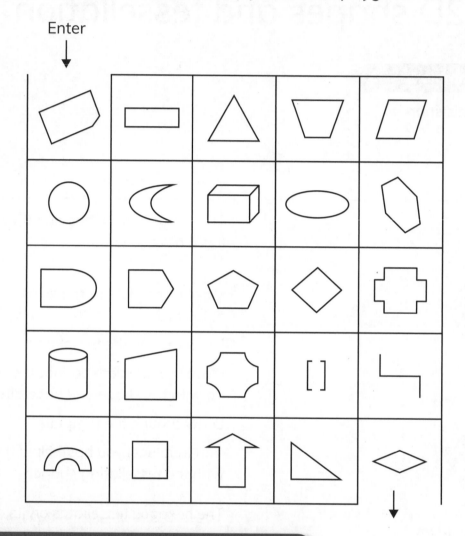

> **Tip**
>
> **Polygon checklist**
>
> A polygon:
>
> - is a 2D shape
> - is a closed shape
> - has only straight sides and no curved sides.

2 Colour the pieces of the tangram you could use to make each shape.

a

b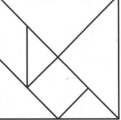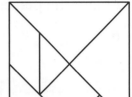

c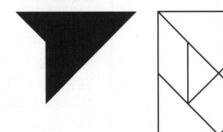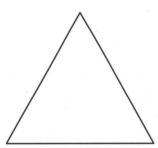

3 Trace this regular triangle and make a template of it from card.

Use your template to tessellate the triangle in the space below.

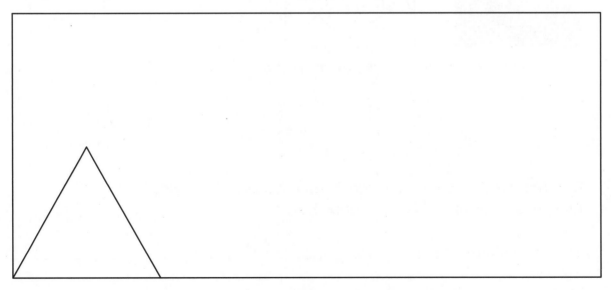

How many triangles fit in the space? _____

Practice

4   Colour the pieces of the tangram you could use to make each shape.

a

 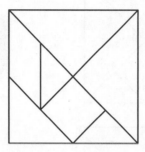

Name the shapes used to make the new shape.

_____   _____

_____   _____

Describe the new shape.

The new shape _____

_____

b

 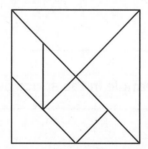

Name the shapes used to make the new shape.

_____   _____   _____

_____   _____

Describe the new shape. Include the number of right angles
and pairs of parallel sides the shape has.

The new shape _____

_____

c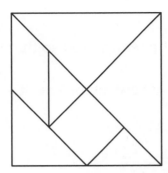

Name the shapes used to make the new shape.

_____   _____   _____

Describe the new shape. Include the number of right angles
and pairs of parallel sides the shape has.

The new shape _____

_____

5 Trace the two shapes in this tessellating pattern. Use your tracing
and a pencil and ruler to continue the pattern to fill the space below.

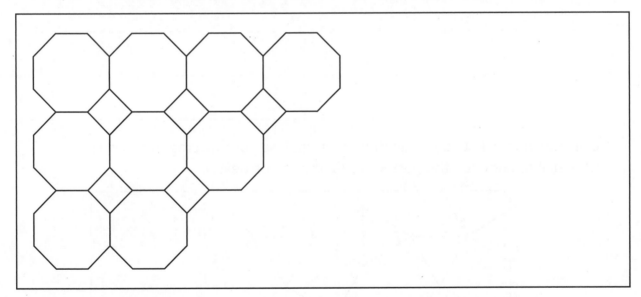

What two shapes make the tessellating pattern?

_____

Challenge

6   How can the pieces of the tangram be rearranged so that they fit exactly into the grey shape?
Draw lines on the grey shape to show how the pieces fit.

Tip

You could trace and cut out the pieces.

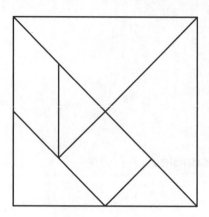
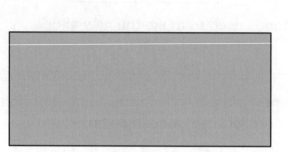

Write four things to describe the properties of the grey shape.

The grey shape:

- _____

- _____

- _____

- _____

7   Trace the shapes in this tessellating pattern. Use your tracing and a ruler and pencil to continue the pattern to fill the space below.

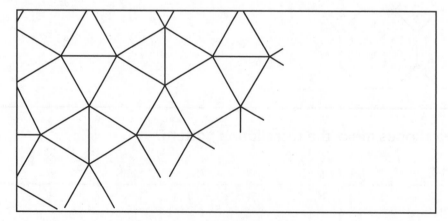

> 6.2 Symmetry

Worked example 2

Find all of the lines of symmetry in this pattern.
How many lines of symmetry does the pattern have?

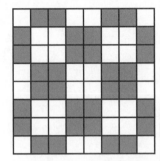

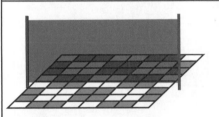

Put your mirror onto the pattern.
The base of the mirror must go
through the middle of the pattern.

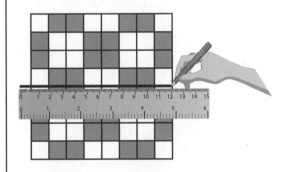

Move the mirror around the shape until the
reflection shows exactly the same pattern as is
on the shape behind the mirror.

Try placing the mirror along the possible vertical
and horizontal lines of symmetry first. Then try
diagonal lines.

When you find a line of symmetry, remove the
mirror and draw the line onto the pattern.

Continue moving the mirror and checking for
lines of symmetry until you have found all
of them. Count the number of lines.

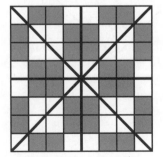

Answer: The pattern has 4 lines of symmetry.

Exercise 6.2

Focus

1   Use a mirror to find all of the lines of symmetry on this pattern.
    Draw the lines of symmetry onto the paper with a ruler.

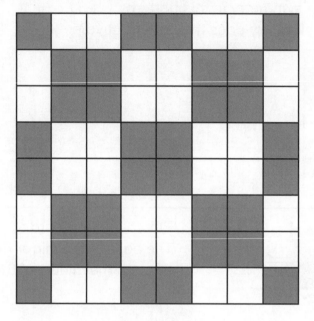

 2   Each of these shapes has one line of symmetry.
    Find and draw the line of symmetry onto the shapes.

  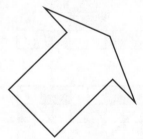

3   This is a square. It has four lines of symmetry.
Draw all of the lines of symmetry onto the square.

Practice

4   Draw all of the lines of symmetry on this square mosaic design.

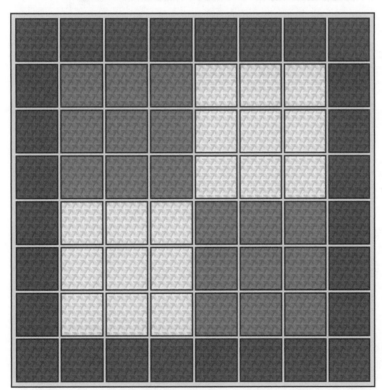

How many lines of symmetry does it have?

_____

5 Copy and complete the table for the octagons.

A 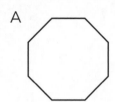   B 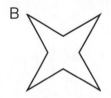   C   D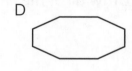

Octagon	Number of lines of symmetry
A	
B	
C	
D	

6 Lines of symmetry have been drawn on this shape.
One of the lines is wrong.
Circle the line that is not a line of symmetry.

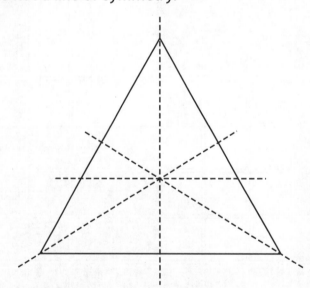

Challenge

 7

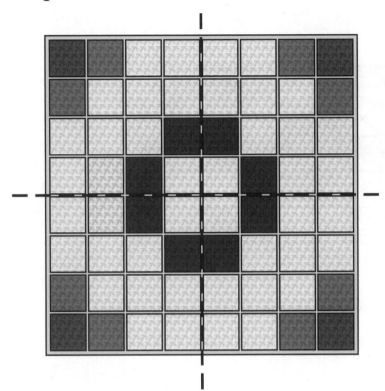

This square mosaic design has a line of horizontal symmetry and a line of vertical symmetry.

a   Draw any other lines of symmetry on the mosaic that you can find.

b   How many lines of symmetry does the mosaic pattern have?

_____

c   If a pattern has a horizontal line of symmetry and a vertical line of symmetry, will it always also have a diagonal line of symmetry?

Explain your reasoning.

_____

_____

_____

8 This rectangular mosaic design has a line of horizontal symmetry and a line of vertical symmetry.

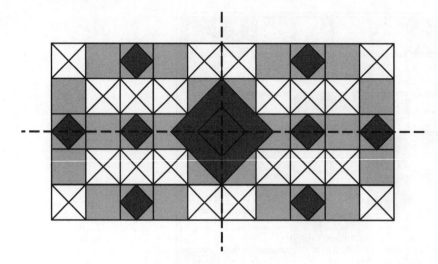

    a Draw any other lines of symmetry on the mosaic that you can see.

    b How many lines of symmetry does the mosaic pattern have?

    _____

9 **a** Draw any lines of symmetry on the mosaic that you can see.

    b How many lines of symmetry does the mosaic pattern have? _____

10 Draw all of the lines of symmetry on these regular polygons.

a

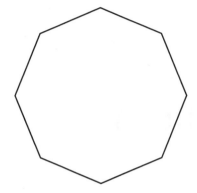

Name of shape: _____

Number of lines of symmetry: _____

b

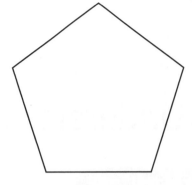

Name of shape: _____

Number of lines of symmetry: _____

c

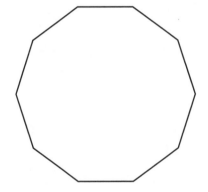

Name of shape: _____

Number of lines of symmetry: _____

7 ▶ Fractions

› 7.1 Understanding fractions

Worked example 1

Tick (✓) all the fractions that have $\frac{1}{4}$ shaded.

A   B 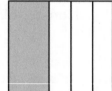   C 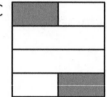   D

Answer:

A    B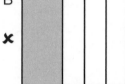

C 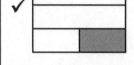   D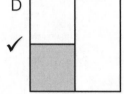

A ✓ 1 part out of 4 equal parts is shaded.

B ✗ The 4 parts are not equal.

C ✓ The 2 shaded parts are equal to 1 large rectangle.

D ✓ The shaded square is one quarter of the total area.

---

denominator   fraction   numerator

Exercise 7.1

Focus

1 Tick (✓) the shapes which have $\frac{1}{2}$ shaded.

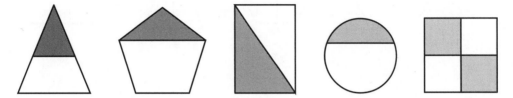

2 Here is part of a number line.
   Write the missing fraction.

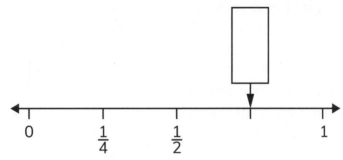

3 The diagrams show fractions with a numerator of 2. The denominators are different.

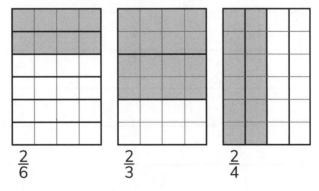

$\frac{2}{6}$ $\frac{2}{3}$ $\frac{2}{4}$

Write fractions to complete the number sentences.

$\frac{2}{4}$ is greater than ☐ $\frac{2}{4}$ is less than ☐

Write the fractions in order, starting with the smallest.

_____

Practice

4 Which shapes have been divided into quarters?

 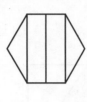

A   B   C   D   E

_____

5 Zina has a jug of water.

a What fraction of a litre of water is in the jug?

_____

b How much water does Zina need to add so that the jug contains 1 litre?

_____

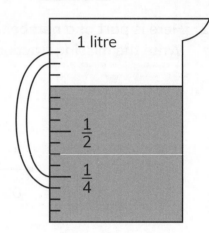

6 Look at the number wall. It is not complete.

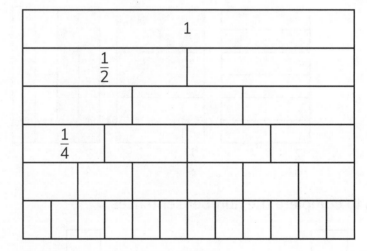

Use it to help you complete the number sentences.
Use the signs > or < .

$\frac{1}{4}$ ⬚ $\frac{1}{6}$ ⬚ $\frac{1}{12}$ $\frac{2}{12}$ ⬚ $\frac{2}{6}$ $\frac{2}{3}$ ⬚ $\frac{2}{12}$

Challenge

7   Shade the given fraction of each of these shapes.

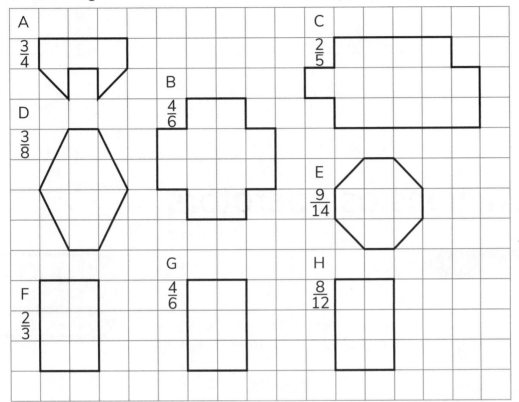

What do you notice about the fractions of F, G and H?

_____

8   Here is a number line.

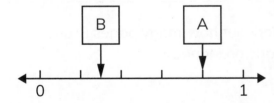

Write the value of A as a fraction. _____

Write the value of B as a fraction. _____

9   Is the following statement always, sometimes or never true?
    If you divide a shape into four parts you have split it into quarters.
    Explain your answer.

_____

_____

> 7.2 Fractions as operators

Worked example 2

There are 40 pages in Bruno's book.

He reads $\frac{1}{5}$ of the book on Monday.

How many pages does he have left to read?

$\frac{1}{5}$ of 40 = 40 ÷ 5	Work out how many pages Bruno reads on Monday.
40 ÷ 5 = 8	
So Bruno has read 8 pages.	
40 − 8 = 32	Subtract to work out how many pages are left.
Answer: Bruno has 32 pages left to read.	

operator

unit fraction

Exercise 7.2

Focus

1   Here are 15 counters. Draw a ring around $\frac{1}{5}$ of them.

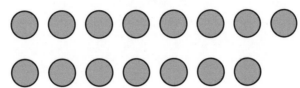

2   What is one sixth of 24?

_____

  3   Draw a line from each calculation to the correct box.

$\frac{1}{2}$ of 20

$\frac{1}{5}$ of 60

$\frac{1}{4}$ of 32

$\frac{1}{3}$ of 30

| Answer less than 10 |
| Answer equal to 10 |
| Answer more than 10 |

4   Leo takes $40 on a shopping trip.

He spends $\frac{1}{5}$ of his money.

How much money does he spend?

_____

5   Use this strip to help you find $\frac{1}{7}$ of 56. You can use the diagram to help you.

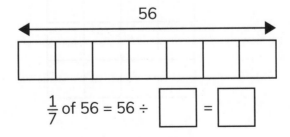

$\frac{1}{7}$ of 56 = 56 ÷ ☐ = ☐

Practice

6   Jamil has 16 cards.
    He gives a quarter of his cards to his friend.
    How many cards has Jamil got left?

    _____

7   Find $\frac{1}{3}$ of 21 cm

    _____

8   Each number in this sequence is a quarter of the number before.

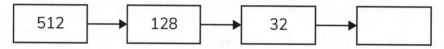

    Write the number in the final box.

 9   Find the odd one out.

    $\frac{1}{3}$ of 6 $\frac{1}{4}$ of 8 $\frac{1}{5}$ of 15 $\frac{1}{6}$ of 12

    Show working to explain your answer.

    _____

    _____

10 Divide the rectangle into four parts.

    The pieces must be $\frac{1}{2}, \frac{1}{4}, \frac{1}{6}$ and $\frac{1}{12}$ of the rectangle.

    They must not overlap.

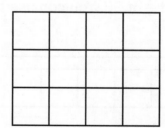

Challenge

11 Parveen has a packet of 20 balloons.

$\frac{1}{4}$ of the balloons are red.

How many balloons are not red?

_____

 12 Nasreen has a packet of coloured beads.
The packet contains 5 orange beads, 5 red beads and 10 blue beads.
Nasreen says, 'Half the beads are blue.'
She is correct. Explain how you know.

_____

_____

13 Look at this pattern.

$\frac{1}{4}$ of 4 = 1 ⟶ $\frac{1}{4}$ of 8 = 2 ⟶ $\frac{1}{4}$ of 12 = 3 ⟶

Write the next three numbers in the sequence.

_____

_____

14 What is the missing number?

$\frac{1}{3}$ of 30 = $\frac{1}{2}$ of $\boxed{}$

 15 Hassan says, 'I would rather have $\frac{1}{3}$ of \$36 than $\frac{1}{4}$ of \$60 because $\frac{1}{3}$ is bigger than $\frac{1}{4}$.'

Do you agree with Hassan? Explain your answer.

_____

_____

_____

8 ▶ Angles

> 8.1 Comparing angles

Worked example 1

Which of these angles is smaller?

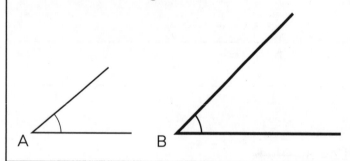

Use tracing paper and a ruler. Trace one of the angles with the tracing paper and a ruler.

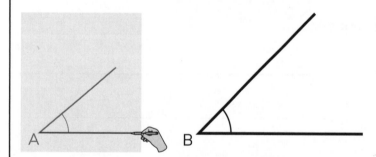

Place the traced angle over the other angle to see which angle is greater.

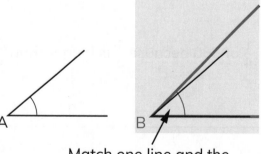

Match one line and the points of the angles

Tip

Notice that the length of the lines and the thickness of the lines do not change the angle.

Answer: Angle A is smaller than angle B.

angle   compare   degrees

Exercise 8.1

Focus

1   Circle the angle that is greater in each pair.

a

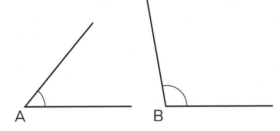

b

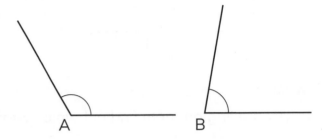

c

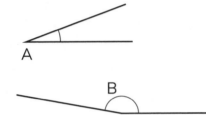

d

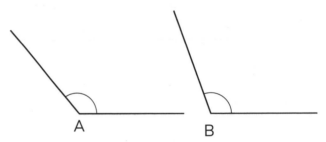

e

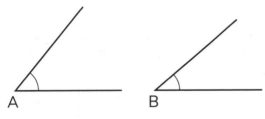

f

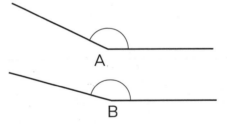

2   These angles are in order from smallest to greatest.
One angle is in the wrong place. Circle the angle in the wrong place.

a

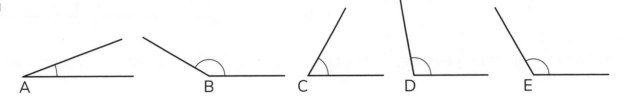

b

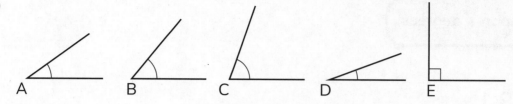

c

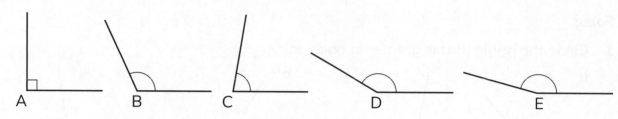

Practice

3 Use tracing paper to find out which angle is smaller. Circle the smaller angle.

a

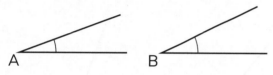

b

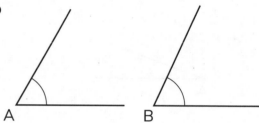

c

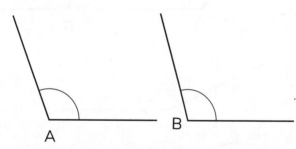

d

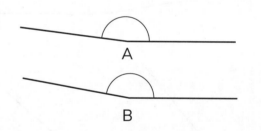

e

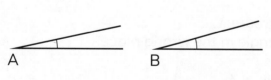

f

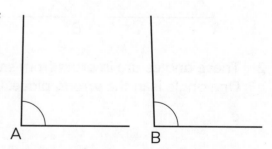

4 Which pair of angles was the most difficult to compare in question 3? Explain why.

_____

_____

5   Use a ruler to draw an angle that is greater than the first angle
    and smaller than the last angle.

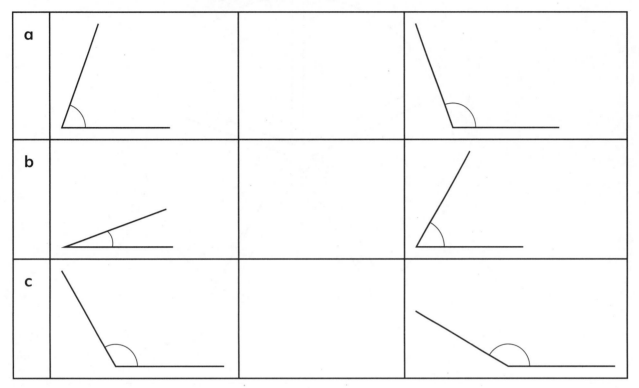

Challenge

6   Put these angles in order from smallest to greatest.

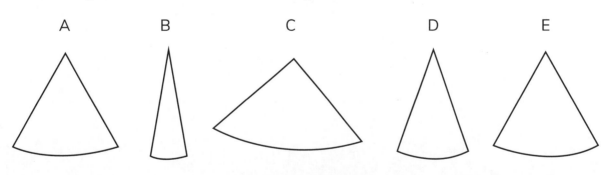

_____

7 Put these angles in order from smallest to greatest.

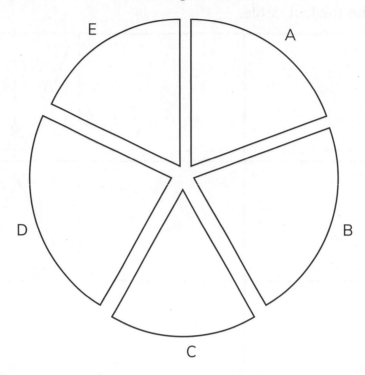

_____

8 Explain in your own words how to compare the sizes of two angles.

_____

_____

_____

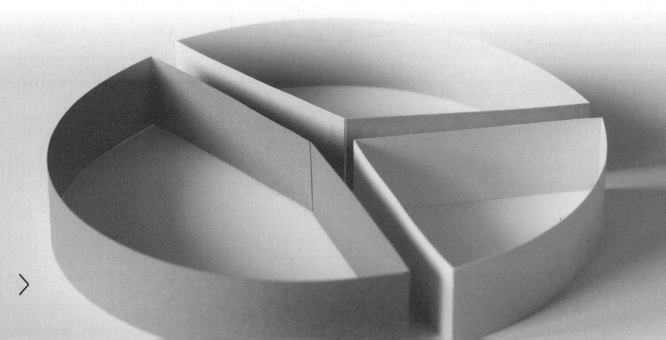

> 8.2 Acute and obtuse

Is this angle acute or obtuse?

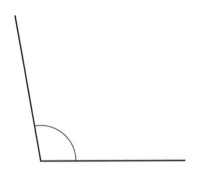

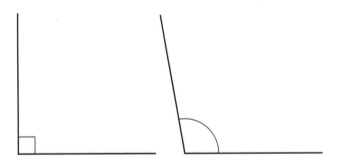

An acute angle is less than 90 degrees, it is less than a right angle or quarter turn.

Compare the angle to a right angle.

The angle is greater than a right angle so it cannot be acute.

0 degrees ——————— Two right angles 180 degrees

The angle is less than two right angles, or half turn.

Compare the angle to two right angles.

An obtuse angle is:

- greater than a right angle
- less than two right angles.

Answer: The angle is obtuse.

acute angle   obtuse angle   right angle

Exercise 8.2

Focus

1   Find the angle words in the word search.

f	p	m	e	o	b	t	u	s	e
w	z	q	s	m	a	l	l	e	r
t	v	c	t	o	a	c	u	t	e
s	w	o	i	f	r	a	w	d	a
u	e	m	m	e	i	c	k	v	v
d	x	p	a	q	g	c	v	z	n
z	a	a	t	k	h	a	j	v	h
k	g	r	e	a	t	e	r	h	g
g	d	e	g	r	e	e	s	i	g
v	j	a	n	g	l	e	b	h	n

acute

angle

compare

degrees

estimate

greater

obtuse

right

smaller

  2   Circle all of the acute angles.

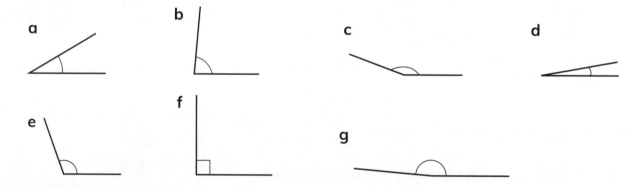

3   This shape has some acute angle corners and some obtuse angle corners.
    Write obtuse or acute to label the other angles of the shape.

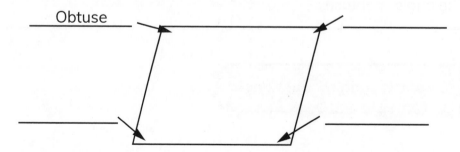

Obtuse

Practice

4   Use a ruler to draw five angles in each box that match the heading.

Acute angles	Obtuse angles

5   The numbers in this grid are all degrees of turn between 0 and 180. Colour a path from the 'start' to the 'end' of the maze. Only pass through squares with a number of degrees that is an obtuse angle. Only move vertically or horizontally.

start 120	45	60	10	50	80	100	130
165	100	175	70	20	150	165	70
35	70	130	40	160	110	10	60
65	80	145	20	70	50	60	30
20	150	160	70	150	120	100	40
50	100	60	20	110	40	160	80
10	170	30	40	135	70	110	145
30	155	125	105	170	60	30	end 120

Challenge

6   a   Draw a triangle that has three acute angles.

    b   Draw a triangle that has a right angle.

    c   Draw a triangle that has an obtuse angle.

    d   Label each angle in your triangles as 'acute', 'obtuse' or 'right angle'.

 7   Write 'obtuse' or 'acute' to complete the sentences.

    a   An _____ angle is between 90 and 180 degrees.

    b   An angle of 59 degrees is _____ .

    c   An _____ angle is smaller than a right angle.

    d   An angle of 100 degrees is _____ .

    e   An _____ angle is between 0 and 90 degrees.

› 8.3 Estimating angles

Worked example 3

estimate

You can use this decision tree and diagram to help you estimate the size of angles.

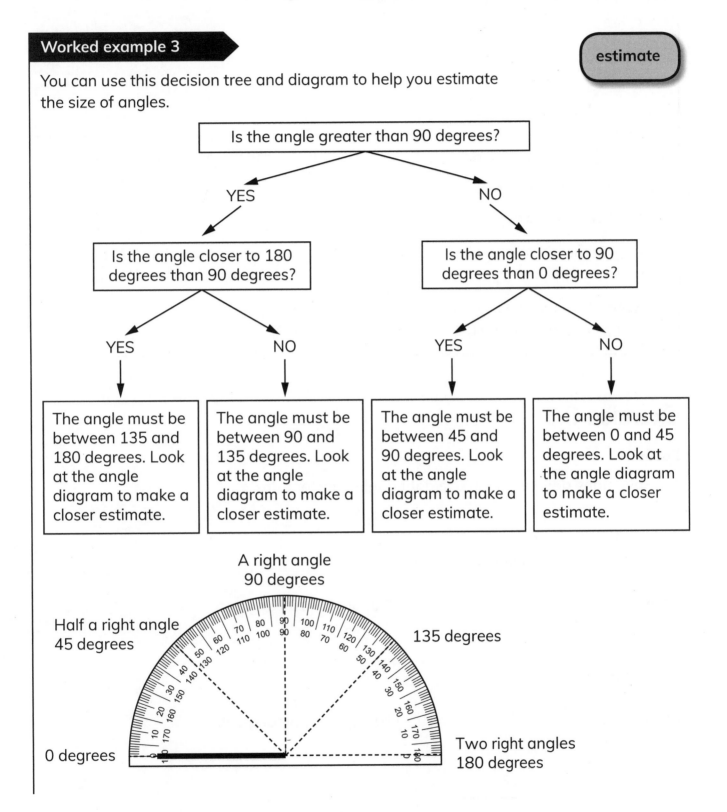

Continued

Estimate the size of this angle in degrees.

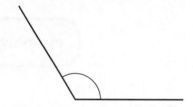

This angle is greater than 90 degrees.	Use the decision tree first.
It is closer to 90 degrees than 180 degrees.	
So, it is between 90 degrees and 135 degrees.	
Looking at the diagram we can estimate that the angle is about 125 degrees.	Then use the diagram to estimate the size of the angle.

Answer: The exact measurement of the angle is 122 degrees.
A good estimate would be between 110 degrees and 130 degrees.

Exercise 8.3

Focus

1   How many degrees are in one right angle quarter turn?

_____

2   Circle the best estimate for each angle.

a
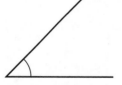
45 degrees / 100 degrees

b
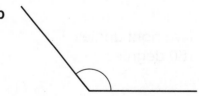
130 degrees / 80 degrees

c   95 degrees / 85 degrees

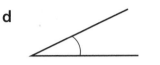

d   30 degrees / 80 degrees

e   110 degrees / 160 degrees

3   Match the label to the angle by estimating the size of the angles.

a   b   d   e

                                c

15 degrees   90 degrees   135 degrees   170 degrees   45 degrees

Practice

4   a   How many right angles do you turn to make a full circle?

_____

b   How many degrees are there in a full circle?

_____

c   How many right angles do you turn to make three-quarters of a circle?

_____

d   How many degrees are there in three-quarters of a circle?

_____

5 Estimate the size of each angle in degrees.

a

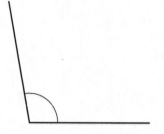

_____

b

_____

c

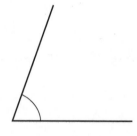

_____

d

_____

e

_____

f

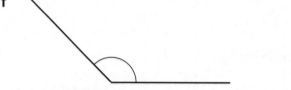

_____

6 Are you better at estimating acute or obtuse angles? Or are you equally good at both? What can you do to help you make better estimates?

_____

_____

_____

Challenge

7   a   Sal turned on the spot 270 degrees. How many right angles is that?

_____

    b   How many more degrees does he need to turn to be back where he started?

_____

8   Describe the relationship between the number of right angles
    and the number of degrees in an angle.

_____

_____

9   Use a ruler and pencil to draw angles that you estimate are close to these labels.

    a   90 degrees   b   45 degrees

    c   20 degrees   d   135 degrees

    e   100 degrees   f   160 degrees

9 ▶ Comparing, rounding and dividing

❯ 9.1 Rounding, ordering and comparing whole numbers

Round 6543 to the nearest 1000.

6543 lies between 6000 and 7000, but it is closer to 7000 than to 6000.

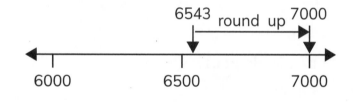

To round to the **nearest thousand**, look at the hundreds digit:

- if it is less than 5 round down
- if it is 5 or more round up.

1000s	100s	10s	1s
6	5	4	3

round up to the next thousand

Answer: 7000

compare   order   round   round to the nearest

Exercise 9.1

Focus

1 2505 = 2510 rounded to the nearest 10.

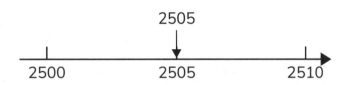

Round these numbers to the nearest 10.

a 3509 = _____ to the nearest 10.

b 3489 = _____ to the nearest 10.

c 4655 = _____ to the nearest 10.

2 Circle all the numbers that round to 90 when rounded to the nearest 10.

85   94   97   82   86

3 Place these numbers in order of size, starting with the smallest.

a 6505   6550   5650   6555   5656

_____

b 1234   2134   2413   1432   2341

_____

4 Use <, > or = to make these number sentences correct.

a 8216 ◯ 8126   b 6031 ◯ 6013

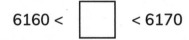 5 What are the even numbers that can go in the box?

6160 < ☐ < 6170

_____

Practice

6 Round these numbers.

 a 3509 = _____ to the nearest 100.

 b 3499 = _____ to the nearest 1000.

 c 4655 = _____ to the nearest 1000.

7 Complete this table.

Number	Rounded to the nearest thousand	Rounded to the nearest hundred	Rounded to the nearest ten
4155			
4505			
5455			

8 3160 < ☐ < 3190

What are the multiples of 10 that can go in the box?

_____

9 Use the digits 2, 3, 5 and 7 to make five different 4-digit numbers.
Use 2, 3, 5 and 7 once in each number.

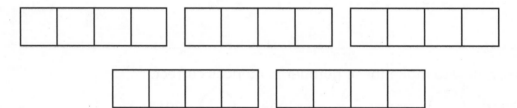

Write the numbers in order, starting with the largest.

_____

10 The highest point in the world is Mount Everest in Nepal at 8848 metres above sea level.

Round 8848 metres to the nearest hundred metres.

_____

11 Round these numbers.

a 3509 = _____ to the nearest 1000.

b 34 999 = _____ to the nearest 10 000.

c 469 543 = _____ to the nearest 100 000.

Challenge

12 The table shows details of five mathematicians.

	Name	Born	Died
A	Leonhard Euler	1707	1783
B	Carl Gauss	1777	1855
C	Ada Lovelace	1815	1852
D	Isaac Newton	1642	1727
E	Alan Turing	1912	1954

You could do some research to find out about the lives of famous mathematicians born in your country.

a Use the timeline to place the mathematicians in order according to the year they were born.

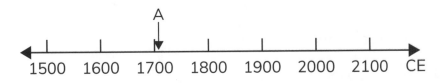

b List the mathematicians in order according to how long they lived.

_____

_____

_____

_____

13 Use the numbers in the boxes to complete the number sentences.
Use each number once.

| 91899 | | 897910 | | 100192 | | 455110 | | 686400 |

455 119 > _____   855 900 < _____   98 150 > _____

500 779 < _____   259 420 > _____

> 9.2 Division of 2-digit numbers

Worked example 2

a The school cook needs 75 cartons of juice.
There are 4 cartons in each pack.
How many packs must the cook buy?

b Amy has 75 cents.
One sweet costs 4 cents.
How many sweets can she buy?

division

divisor

remainder

round down

round up

The first step in both questions is to work out $75 \div 4$.

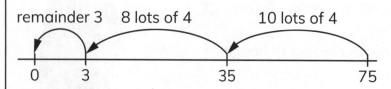

remainder 3   8 lots of 4   10 lots of 4

0   3   35   75

$75 \div 4 = 18 \text{ r } 3$

Answer:

a You must round up: 18 packs does not give enough cartons.

The cook must buy 19 packs.

b You must round down: Amy does not have enough money to buy 19 sweets.

Amy can buy 18 sweets.

Exercise 9.2

Focus

1 Complete the remainder chart for 24.
The first one has been done for you.

24 divided by	2	3	4	5	6	7	8	9	10
Remainder	0								

Describe your results.

_____

_____

2 A jug holds 2 litres.
Ali needs 26 litres of apple juice for her party.
How many jugs of apple juice must Ali make?

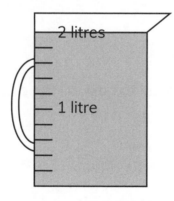

_____

3 Work out these calculations. Show your method.
Remember to estimate before you calculate.

a   91 ÷ 7   b   96 ÷ 8

_____   _____

4   Ali buys 48 tennis balls.
    The balls are in packs of 3.
    How many packs does Ali buy?

_____

 5   Write the missing numbers.

$8 ÷ 2 = \boxed{} ÷ 4 = 32 ÷ \boxed{}$

Practice

6   There are 22 pencils in a pot.
    How many children can have 3 pencils each?

_____

7   Roz bakes 62 cakes.
    She packs the cakes in boxes.
    Each box holds 8 cakes.
    How many boxes does she need to pack all the cakes?

_____

8   Paul wants to put 52 photos in an album.
    A full page holds 6 photos.
    He fills as many whole pages as possible.
    How many photos are left over?

_____

9 Here are four numbers.

65   75   85   95

Divide each number by 7.
Circle the number that leaves a remainder of 1.

10 Which pairs of numbers can be written in the boxes?

$36 \div \boxed{} = \boxed{}$

_____

Challenge

11 Pierre wants to buy a bike.
The bike costs $97.
Pierre saves $10 every Saturday.
How many Saturdays will it take him to save enough money to buy the bike?

_____

12 Use the code to find the name of the planet.

Remainder	1	2	3	4	5	6	7	8	9
Letter	Y	E	T	M	A	R	S	C	U

$29 \div 5$ $47 \div 3$ $76 \div 7$ $98 \div 9$ $19 \div 10$ $83 \div 7$ $47 \div 2$

_____

13 Find the rule, then complete these division wheels.

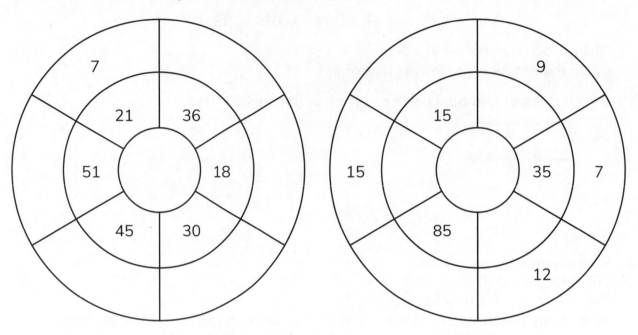

14 Draw a line to join each division question to the correct rounding operation.

Coconuts cost $2 each. How many coconuts can be bought for $15?

14 peaches are put in bags. Each bag holds 4 peaches. How many full bags are there?

A minibus holds 12 people. 50 people go on an outing. How many minibuses are needed?

Round up

Round down

 15 Which pairs of numbers could be written in the boxes?

60 ÷ ☐ = ☐

10 ▶ Collecting and recording data

❭ 10.1 How to collect and record data

Worked example 1

This data shows the number of bicycles owned by some families.

5, 1, 3, 2, 3, 0, 2, 4, 1, 2, 2, 0, 0

Record the data using a dot plot.

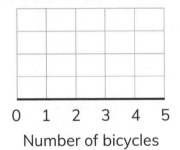

0   1   2   3   4   5
Number of bicycles

Draw an axis long enough to show all the numbers in the set of data. Label the axis.

It is best to use squared paper to make it easier to space the dots evenly.

Answer:

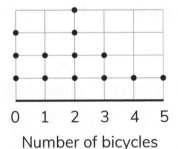

0   1   2   3   4   5
Number of bicycles

Draw one dot above the number on the axis for each time the number appears in the data.

For example, there are two families with 1 bicycle, so show two dots above 1.

data   dot plot   statistical question

Exercise 10.1

Focus

1   Ingrid counted the birds in her garden each day.
    Complete the table to show how many days she saw each number of birds.

3, 3, 4, 4, 4, 5, 5, 5, 5, 6, 6, 7, 7, 8

Number of birds	How many days?
3	2
4	
5	
6	
7	
8	

> **Tip**
>
> In the list there are two days when Ingrid saw 3 birds. The number 2 goes in the table next to 3 birds.

2   Billy looked in 15 packets of sweets and counted the red sweets
    he found in each packet.
    He used a dot plot to record how many red sweets he found.

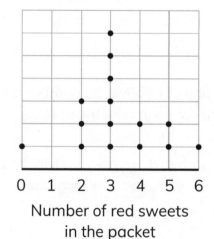

Number of red sweets
in the packet

a   How many packets had 0 red sweets?

    _____

b   How many packets had 3 red sweets?

    _____

c   What is the greatest number of red sweets
    that Billy found?

    _____

3 Billy counted the green sweets in the packets.
   This is how many green sweets he found in each packet.

   1, 1, 2, 2, 2, 2, 3, 3, 3, 4, 6, 6, 6, 7, 8

   Complete the dot plot with the number of green sweets he found in the packets.

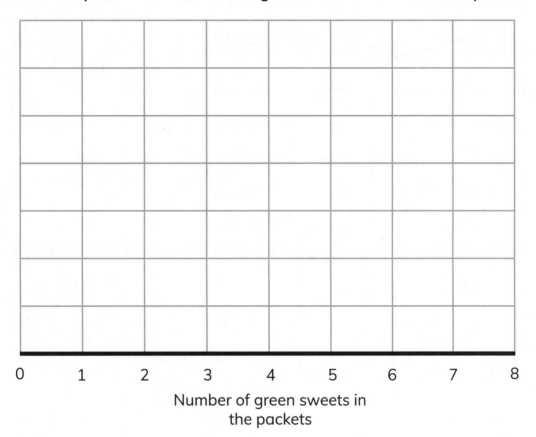

Number of green sweets in
the packets

4 Complete these sentences and choose the words to plan an investigation
   to find out how many seeds there are in a packet.

   Question: How many _____ are there in a packet?

   I will **count / collect** how many seeds are in each packet.

   I will **plant / record** the number of seeds in a _____ .

Practice

5   Aron counted the number of cars that passed his window each hour.

a   Complete the table to show his results.

10, 11, 14, 10, 10, 13, 14, 13, 13, 13, 11, 13

Number of cars	How many hours?

b   Complete the dot plot to show the number of cars that passed each hour.

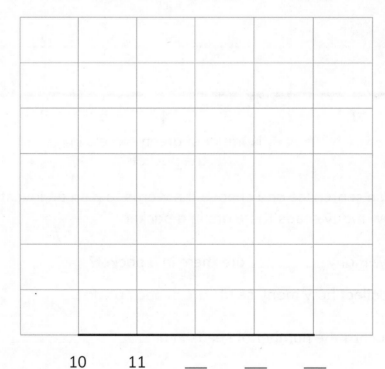

10   11   ___   ___   ___

Number of   _____

6   Use the table or the dot plot in Question 5 to answer these questions.

   a   For how many hours did Aron see 12 cars?

   _____

   b   What was the greatest number of cars Aron saw in an hour?

   _____

   c   For how many hours did Aron see less than 12 cars?

   _____

   d   Did you use the table or the dot plot?

   _____

   Why?

   _____

   _____

7   You are going to plan an investigation to find out how many cubes your friends can hold in one hand.

   Complete the plan.

   Question: How many _____?

   People I will use: _____

I will record the data in this table.

Number of _____	Number of _____

Carry out the investigation and complete the table.

Challenge

8 Nasreen counted the number of seeds in 12 packets of sunflower seeds. This is the number of seeds in each packet:

23, 24, 22, 22, 22, 23, 26, 24, 24, 21, 23, 23

   a   Draw a table to show how many packets had each number of seeds.

b Draw a dot plot to show how many seeds are in each packet.

c How many packets had 25 seeds?

_____

d What was the least number of seeds found in a packet?

_____

e How many packets had more than 23 seeds in them?

_____

f Reflect on how you answered questions c, d and e.
Did you use the table or the dot plot?

_____

Why?

_____

_____

9 You are going to plan an investigation to find out how many cubes your friends can connect together in a line in one minute.

Complete the plan.

Question: _____ ?

People I will use: _____

Equipment I will need: _____

Use the space below to collect your data.
Then use the grid below to represent your data in a dot plot.

11 ▶ Fractions and percentages

❯ 11.1 Equivalence, comparing and ordering fractions

Worked example 1

Put the correct sign < or > between this pair of fractions.

$$\frac{3}{4} \quad \boxed{} \quad \frac{5}{8}$$

> equivalent fraction
>
> proper fraction

$\frac{3}{4} = \frac{6}{8}$ Change $\frac{3}{4}$ into an equivalent fraction in eighths.

$\frac{6}{8} > \frac{5}{8}$ Compare the two fractions and write the correct sign.

Answer: $\frac{3}{4} > \frac{5}{8}$

Exercise 11.1

Focus

1 Here is a table. The rows for the 1× table and the 5× table are in grey.

×	1	2	3	4	5	6	7	8	9	10
1	1	2	3	4	5	6	7	8	9	10
2	2	4	6	8	10	12	14	16	18	20
3	3	6	9	12	15	18	21	24	27	30
4	4	8	12	16	20	24	28	32	36	40
5	5	10	15	20	25	30	35	40	45	50
6	6	12	18	24	30	36	42	48	54	60
7	7	14	21	28	35	42	49	56	63	70
8	8	16	24	32	40	48	56	64	72	80
9	9	18	27	36	45	54	63	72	81	90
10	10	20	30	40	50	60	70	80	90	100

You can use the table to help work out equivalent fractions:

$$\frac{1}{5} = \frac{2}{10} = \frac{3}{15} = \frac{4}{20} = \frac{5}{25} = \frac{6}{30} = \frac{7}{35} = \frac{8}{40} = \frac{9}{45} = \frac{10}{50}$$

Use the table to complete these equivalent fractions.

a $\frac{1}{2} = \frac{2}{\square} = \frac{\square}{6} = \frac{4}{\square} = \frac{\square}{10} = \frac{6}{\square} = \frac{\square}{14} = \frac{8}{\square} = \frac{\square}{18} = \frac{10}{\square}$

b $\quad \dfrac{3}{4} = \dfrac{\square}{8} = \dfrac{9}{\square} = \dfrac{\square}{16} = \dfrac{15}{\square} = \dfrac{\square}{24} = \dfrac{21}{\square} = \dfrac{\square}{32} = \dfrac{27}{\square} = \dfrac{\square}{40}$

c $\quad \dfrac{2}{3} = \dfrac{4}{\square} = \dfrac{\square}{9} = \dfrac{8}{\square} = \dfrac{\square}{15} = \dfrac{12}{\square} = \dfrac{\square}{21} = \dfrac{16}{\square} = \dfrac{\square}{27} = \dfrac{20}{\square}$

Use the fraction wall to help you answer questions 2 and 3.

1							
$\frac{1}{2}$				$\frac{1}{2}$			
$\frac{1}{3}$		$\frac{1}{3}$			$\frac{1}{3}$		
$\frac{1}{4}$		$\frac{1}{4}$		$\frac{1}{4}$		$\frac{1}{4}$	
$\frac{1}{6}$	$\frac{1}{6}$	$\frac{1}{6}$	$\frac{1}{6}$	$\frac{1}{6}$	$\frac{1}{6}$		
$\frac{1}{8}$	$\frac{1}{8}$	$\frac{1}{8}$	$\frac{1}{8}$	$\frac{1}{8}$	$\frac{1}{8}$	$\frac{1}{8}$	$\frac{1}{8}$

2 Write each set of fractions in order, smallest first.
Write down the equivalent fractions you use to work out each answer.

a $\quad \dfrac{2}{3}, \dfrac{3}{4}, \dfrac{1}{3}, \dfrac{5}{8}$ _____

b $\quad \dfrac{2}{3}, \dfrac{5}{6}, \dfrac{1}{2}, \dfrac{7}{8}$ _____

3 Put the correct sign < or > between each pair of fractions.

a $\quad \dfrac{1}{2} \;\square\; \dfrac{5}{8}$ $\qquad\qquad\qquad\qquad$ b $\quad \dfrac{2}{3} \;\square\; \dfrac{5}{6}$

Practice

4   Colour in red the squares containing fractions equivalent to $\frac{2}{3}$.

What letter can you see? _____

Colour in blue the squares containing fractions equivalent to $\frac{3}{4}$.

What letter can you see? _____

$\frac{8}{12}$	$\frac{5}{6}$	$\frac{18}{27}$	$\frac{6}{20}$	$\frac{9}{12}$	$\frac{15}{20}$	$\frac{30}{40}$
$\frac{2}{3}$	$\frac{10}{12}$	$\frac{10}{15}$	$\frac{10}{25}$	$\frac{18}{24}$	$\frac{3}{10}$	$\frac{21}{28}$
$\frac{14}{21}$	$\frac{6}{9}$	$\frac{22}{33}$	$\frac{30}{100}$	$\frac{12}{16}$	$\frac{27}{36}$	$\frac{3}{4}$
$\frac{20}{30}$	$\frac{1}{2}$	$\frac{16}{24}$	$\frac{9}{36}$	$\frac{24}{32}$	$\frac{1}{4}$	$\frac{6}{12}$
$\frac{4}{6}$	$\frac{20}{24}$	$\frac{12}{18}$	$\frac{2}{5}$	$\frac{6}{8}$	$\frac{4}{10}$	$\frac{18}{36}$

5   Here are three fractions.

$$\frac{2}{3} \qquad \frac{1}{4} \qquad \frac{2}{5}$$

Write each fraction in the correct box on the number line.

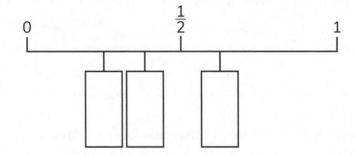

6   Which is larger?

a $\frac{5}{8}$ or $\frac{3}{4}$ _____

b $\frac{5}{6}$ or $\frac{2}{3}$ _____

c $\frac{1}{2}$ or $\frac{3}{8}$ _____

7 Choose different numbers for each numerator to make this number sentence correct.

$$\frac{\square}{8} > \frac{\square}{4}$$

How many different answers can you find?
Both fractions must be less than 1.

_____

_____

Challenge

8 Find sets of three equivalent fractions.

$\frac{3}{4}$	$\frac{5}{6}$	$\frac{6}{20}$	$\frac{8}{12}$	$\frac{4}{10}$
$\frac{2}{3}$	$\frac{10}{12}$	$\frac{6}{8}$	$\frac{10}{25}$	$\frac{3}{10}$
$\frac{20}{24}$	$\frac{4}{6}$	$\frac{30}{100}$	$\frac{9}{12}$	$\frac{2}{5}$

List your sets here:

_____

_____

_____

9 Which is the odd one out? Explain your answer.

$$\frac{9}{12} \qquad \frac{10}{15} \qquad \frac{2}{3}$$

Find more than one answer.

_____

_____

10 △ and ◯ stand for two different numbers.

△ is a multiple of 5

◯ is a multiple of 6

$$\frac{\triangle}{\bigcirc} = \frac{2}{3}$$

What numbers could △ and ◯ stand for?

_____

11 Circle the fraction that is greater than $\frac{1}{2}$ but less than $\frac{3}{4}$.

$$\frac{3}{8} \qquad \frac{2}{4} \qquad \frac{5}{8} \qquad \frac{7}{8}$$

12 Alana says, '$\frac{4}{7}$ is greater than $\frac{4}{9}$.'

Is Alana correct?

Explain how you know.

_____

_____

〉 11.2 Percentages

Worked example 2

a Shade 10% of each grid in grey.

b Shade $\frac{1}{4}$ of each grid in black.

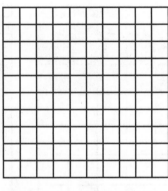

percent

percentage

a 10% = 10 out of 100

There are 100 squares in each grid.

Shade 10 squares grey.

b $\frac{1}{4}$ = 25% = 25 out of 100

Shade 25 squares black.

It does not matter which squares you shade as long as you shade the correct number.

Answer:

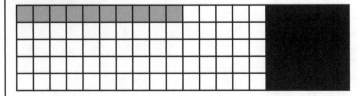

Exercise 11.2

Focus

1   Write the percentage that is coloured in grey.

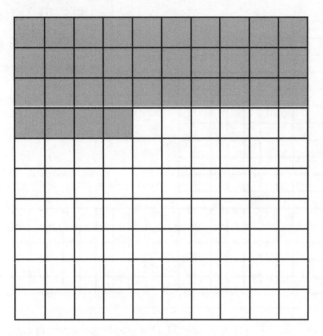 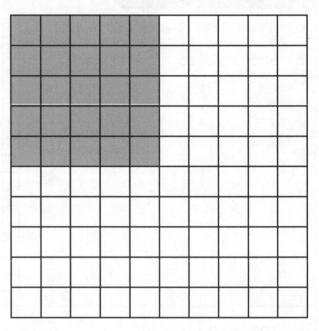

_____   _____

2   Colour these diagrams to show the following percentages.

a   50%

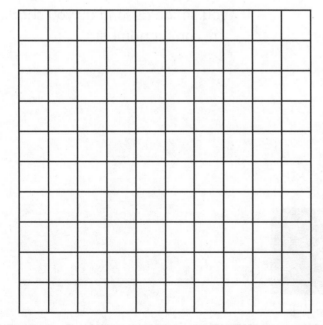

b 75%

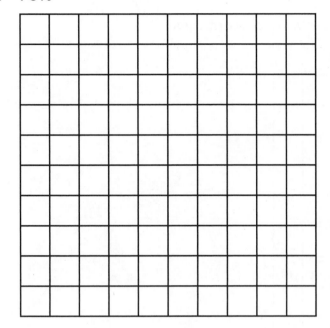

c 10%

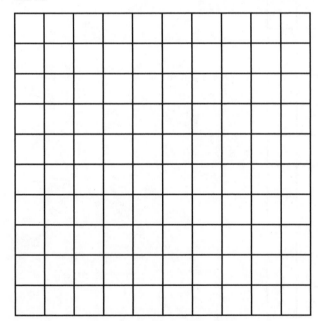

3 Write these fractions as percentages.

a 35 out of 100 = _____ %

b 36 out of 100 = _____ %

c 72 out of 100 = _____ %

d 14 out of 100 = _____ %

e 67 out of 100 = _____ %

Practice

4   Colour these diagrams to show the following percentages.

   a   55%

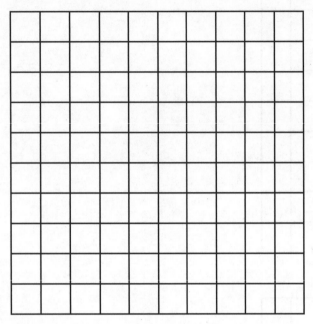

   b   48%

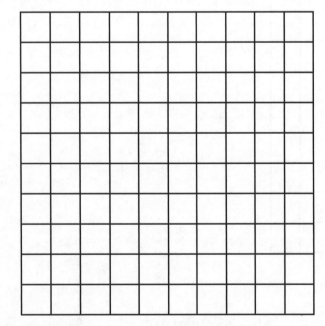

c 1%

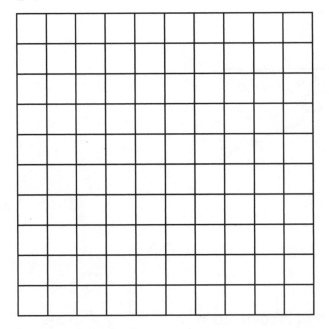

5 Join pairs of shapes that make a whole circle.
You will need to work out the percentage for one of the circles.

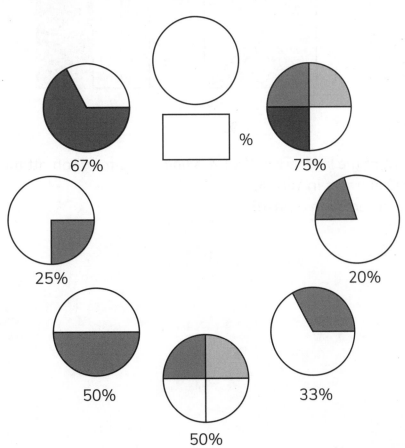

6   Zhen looks at the label in her coat.
    The coat is made of wool and cotton.
    Part of the label is missing.

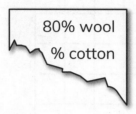

    What percentage of the coat is cotton?

    _____

Challenge

7   Write the percentage of each shape that is coloured in.

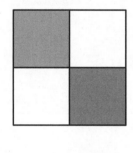   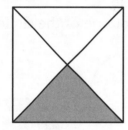   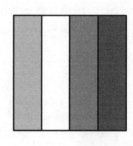   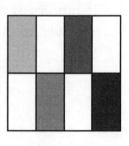

    _____ %   _____ %   _____ %   _____ %

8   Eighty percent of the learners in Year 4 won a prize for good attitude in all lessons.
    There are 100 learners in Year 4.
    How many learners won a prize?

    _____

9   The table shows the colours of flowers in a garden.

Colour	Percentage of flowers
red	
yellow	50%
pink	
white	20%

The percentage of red and pink flowers is the same.
What percentage of the flowers are pink?

_____

10 Colour 25% of each of these grids.

a
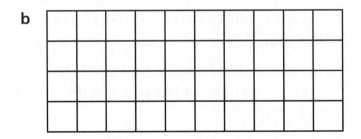

b

12 ▶ Investigating 3D shapes and nets

❯ 12.1 The properties of 3D shapes

Worked example 1

Draw arrows from the words to the parts of the shape.

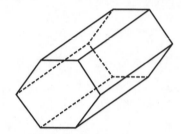

Face

Edge

Vertex

Answer:

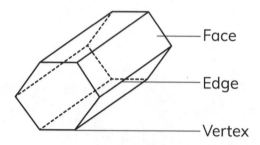

Face

Edge

Vertex

Faces are the flat surfaces of a 3D shape. This rectangle is a flat surface on the hexagonal prism.

Edges are the lines where two faces meet. This line is where two faces meet on the hexagonal prism.

Vertices are the points where edges meet. Three edges meet at this point on the hexagonal prism.

---

cone   edge   face   prism   pyramid   tetrahedron   vertex / vertices

Exercise 12.1

Focus

1   Draw arrows from the words to the parts of this shape.

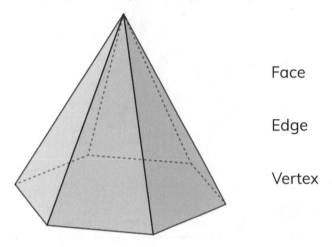

Face

Edge

Vertex

2   This is a cuboid.

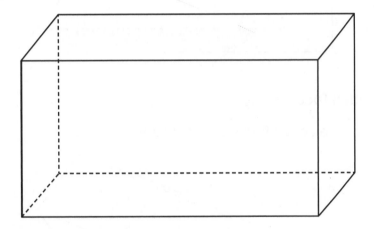

Mark the edges with a green line.

Mark the vertices with a red circle.

a   How many edges are there? _____

b   How many vertices are there? _____

c   How many faces are there? _____

3 a This is a pentagon-based pyramid.

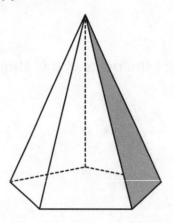

Name the shaded face. _____

b This is a triangular prism.

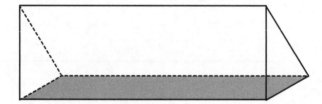

Name the shaded face. _____

4 Write the names of the seven faces of a pentagonal prism

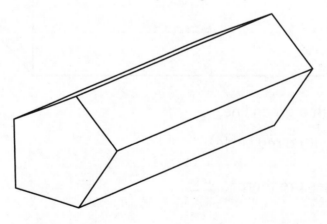

_____   _____   _____   _____

_____   _____   _____

Practice

5 Complete these sentences about the tetrahedron.

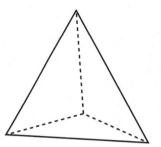

A tetrahedron has:

_____ faces, _____ edges and _____ vertices.

6 This is a face from one of these shapes.

Tick the shapes it could belong to.

A
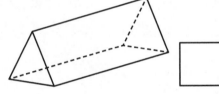

B

C

D
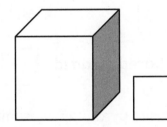

E
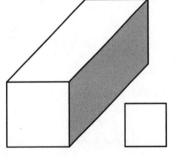

7 Name a 3D shape with more than two triangular faces.

_____

8 Name a 3D shape with a circular face.

_____

Challenge

9   Complete the table to show how many faces, edges and vertices each shape has.

Shape	Number of faces	Number of edges	Number of vertices
Cuboid	6	12	
Triangular prism			6
Pentagon-based pyramid			
Hexagonal prism			
	5	8	5

10 This is a face from one of the shapes in the list.

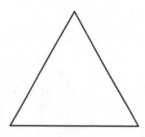

Tick the shapes it could belong to.

Cube ☐   Triangular prism ☐   Tetrahedron ☐

Hexagonal prism ☐   Square-based pyramid ☐

11 Describe how triangular prisms and triangle-based pyramids are similar and different.

_____

_____

_____

› 12.2 Nets of 3D shapes

Worked example 2

What shape does this net make?

A   A tetrahedron

B   A square-based pyramid

C   A cube

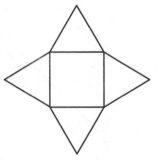

net   tetrahedron

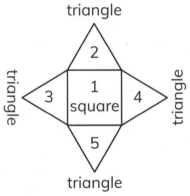

First label the number of faces and the shape of the faces.

This net has 5 faces. It has 1 square face and 4 triangular faces.

This net has 1 square face and 4 triangular faces. The square face must be the base.

The net cannot make a cube.

Check if the shape will be a prism or a pyramid.

- A prism has two opposite faces connected by rectangles.

- A pyramid has a base shape and all other faces are triangles that meet at a vertex.

Answer:

B. This is the net of a square-based pyramid.

Exercise 12.2

Focus

1 Circle the net that will make a hexagonal prism.

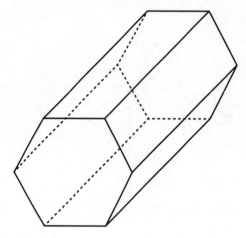

A

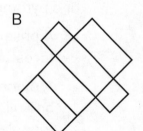

B

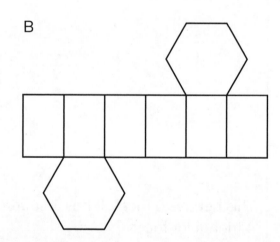

2 All of these nets are the same except one. Circle the odd one out.

A 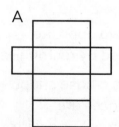   B 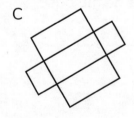   C   D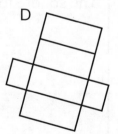

3   Circle the shape that can be made with this net.

Cube   Triangular prism   Pentagon-based pyramid

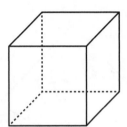   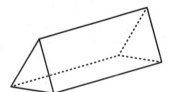   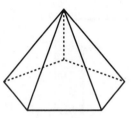

Practice

4   Copy this net onto card and cut it out. Fold it into a 3D shape.
    What 3D shape have you made?

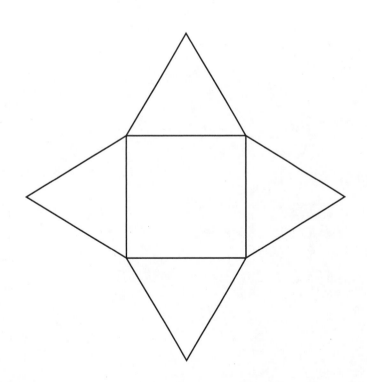

5 Circle the net that will make a triangular prism.

A

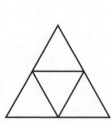

B

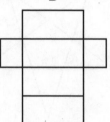
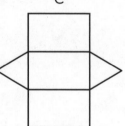

C

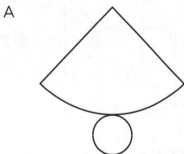

6 Draw lines to match the shape to its net.

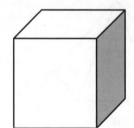

cube

A

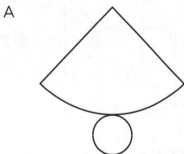

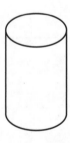

cylinder

B

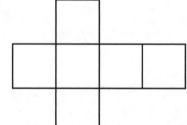

cone

C

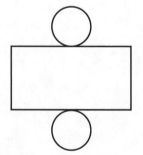

7 Tick the shape that can be made with this net.

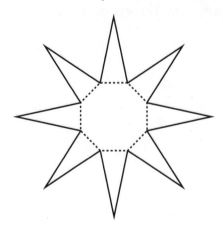

A cube ☐

An octagonal prism ☐

An octagon-based pyramid ☐

Challenge

8 Draw lines to match the shape to its net.

cuboid

A
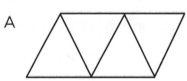

B
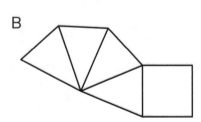

tetrahedron

heptagonal prism

C
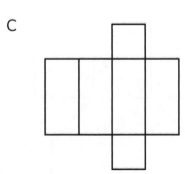

D
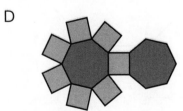

square-based pyramid

9 Arnold has drawn this net to make a pentagon-based pyramid.
Explain how you know that this net will not make a pentagon-based pyramid.

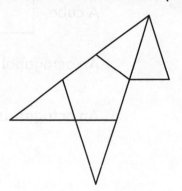

_____

_____

10 Write the name of the shape that this net makes.

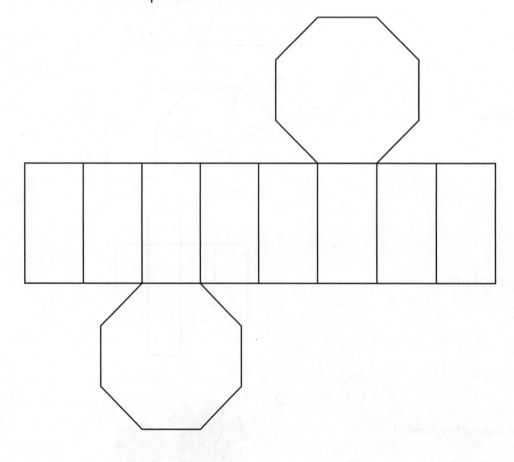

_____

13 ▶ Addition and subtraction

> 13.1 Adding and subtracting efficiently

Worked example 1

Work out 367 + 185.

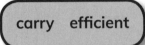

carry   efficient

Method 1:

	100s	10s	0s
	3	6	7
+	1	8	5
		1	2
	1	4	0
	4	0	0
	5	5	2

- Write the numbers in columns.
- Add the ones, then the tens, then the hundreds.
- 7 + 5 = 12
- 60 + 80 = 140
- 300 + 100 = 400
- Add these totals to get the answer:

  400 + 140 + 12 is 552

Method 2:

	100s	10s	0s
	3	6	7
+	1	8	5
	5	5	2
	1	1	

You can write the calculation more efficiently by 'carrying' the tens and hundreds.

- 7 + 5 is 12.
  Record 2 ones and carry 1 ten.
- 60 + 80 + 10 is 150.
  Record 5 tens and carry 1 hundred.
- 300 + 100 + 100 is 500.
  Record 5 hundreds.

Answer: 552

Exercise 13.1

Focus

1   There are 215 girls and 259 boys in the school hall.
    How many boys and girls are in the hall altogether?

_____

2   Look at this diagram.

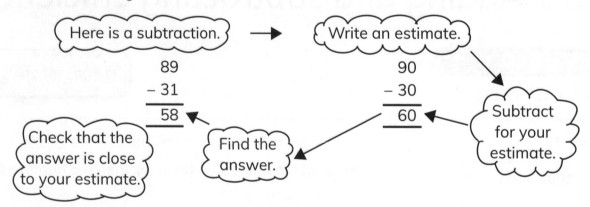

Do the same for these calculations.

a   128 – 62   b   358 – 254   c   548 – 392

_____   _____   _____

 3   Chloe has three digit cards.

She makes the largest number she can with the three cards.
Then she makes the smallest number she can with the three cards.
What is the difference between the two numbers Chloe makes?

_____

4   649 people go to a concert.
    290 people are women.
    312 people are men.
    How many children are at the concert?

_____

Practice

5   The table shows the distance in kilometres between five towns
    in the United Kingdom.

	Birmingham	Cardiff	London	Manchester	Newcastle
Birmingham		179	188	127	334
Cardiff	179		269	278	489
London	188	269		298	441
Manchester	127	278	298		212
Newcastle	334	489	441	212	

> **Tip**
>
> Make sure you can read the table correctly by finding the distance from London to Cardiff. You should find it is 269 kilometres.

a   Nami travels from Birmingham to Manchester and then
    from Manchester to Newcastle.
    How many kilometres does she travel altogether?

_____

b   Raphael travels from London to Birmingham and then
    from Birmingham to Newcastle.
    How many kilometres does he travel altogether?

_____

6 Subtract the largest 2-digit number from 200.

_____

 7 Use only the digits 4 and 5 to complete this calculation.
You may use the digits more than once.

$$\boxed{\,\boxed{}\,\boxed{}} + \boxed{\,\boxed{}} = 500$$

8 Darius spilt ink on his work.
His answer is correct.
What is the missing digit?

$$
\begin{array}{r}
7\quad 3\quad 2 \\
-\ 3\quad \blacksquare\quad 9 \\
\hline
4\quad 1\quad 3 \\
\hline
\end{array}
$$

_____

Challenge

9 Write the missing digits.

	5		9
+	1	9	3
		4	2

10 Use each of the digits 4, 5, 6, 7, 8, 9 in each calculation to make these number sentences true.

$$\boxed{\,\boxed{}\,\boxed{}} - \boxed{\,\boxed{}\,\boxed{}} = 333$$

$$\boxed{\,\boxed{}\,\boxed{}} - \boxed{\,\boxed{}\,\boxed{}} = 111$$

11 What total closest to 800 can you make using two of these numbers?

605	402	503	789
395	899	901	197

_____

12 Last year there were 82 girls and 93 boys in Year 4.
This year there are 190 students in Year 4.
Of these students, 95 are boys.
How many more girls are in Year 4 this year than last year?

_____

 13 Find five pairs of numbers that add up to 900.

545	238	86	228
96	791	355	601
672	109	589	437
463	322	814	465

One has been done for you.

672 + 228 = 900

_____   _____

_____   _____

> 13.2 Adding and subtracting fractions with the same denominator

> **Worked example 2**
>
> Find the missing fraction.
>
> $$\frac{3}{11} + \frac{1}{11} + \boxed{} = \frac{14}{11}$$
>
> ---
>
> Calculate $\frac{3}{11} + \frac{1}{11} = \frac{4}{11}$
>
> The number sentence can then be written as
>
> $$\frac{4}{11} + \boxed{} = \frac{14}{11}$$
>
> So $\boxed{} = \frac{10}{11}$ which can be found by counting on from $\frac{4}{11}$ to $\frac{14}{11}$.
>
> **Answer:** $\frac{10}{11}$

improper fraction

proper fraction

Exercise 13.2

Focus

1   Jamila has cycled $\frac{3}{4}$ of the way to the gym.

What fraction of the distance does she still have to go?

_____

2　Draw lines between two fractions that total 1.
　　Find all the pairs that total 1.

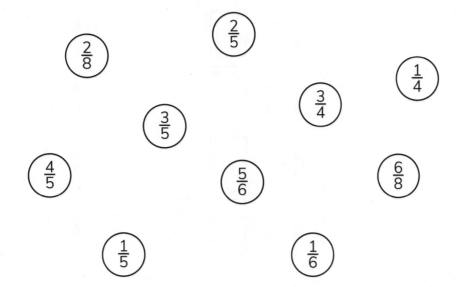

3　Work out these calculations.

a　$\dfrac{5}{6} + \dfrac{3}{6} = \boxed{}$

b　$\dfrac{7}{8} - \dfrac{3}{8} = \boxed{}$

c　$\dfrac{11}{12} - \dfrac{3}{12} = \boxed{}$

d　$\dfrac{7}{12} - \dfrac{5}{12} = \boxed{}$

4　Write the missing numbers.

a　$\dfrac{3}{8} + \boxed{} = \dfrac{9}{8}$　　　b　$\dfrac{6}{8} - \boxed{} = \dfrac{1}{8}$

5　Find the missing fraction.

$\dfrac{3}{8} + \dfrac{1}{8} + \boxed{} = \dfrac{7}{8}$

Practice

6 Write the missing numbers.

$\frac{2}{7} + \frac{6}{7} =$ ☐

$\frac{3}{4} + \frac{3}{4} =$ ☐

$\frac{5}{9} + \frac{7}{9} =$ ☐

$\frac{2}{3} + \frac{2}{3} =$ ☐

$\frac{7}{8} + \frac{6}{8} =$ ☐

$\frac{3}{6} + \frac{4}{6} =$ ☐

$\frac{4}{5} - \frac{1}{5} =$ ☐

$\frac{6}{9} - \frac{3}{9} =$ ☐

$\frac{5}{7} - \frac{2}{7} =$ ☐

$\frac{9}{10} - \frac{1}{10} =$ ☐

$\frac{4}{9} - \frac{1}{9} =$ ☐

$\frac{7}{8} - \frac{2}{8} =$ ☐

7 Write the missing fraction.

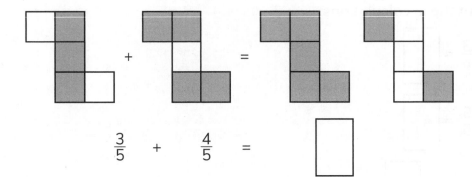

$\frac{3}{5}$ + $\frac{4}{5}$ = ☐

8 Draw lines between two fractions that total $\frac{10}{9}$.

Find all the pairs that total $\frac{10}{9}$.

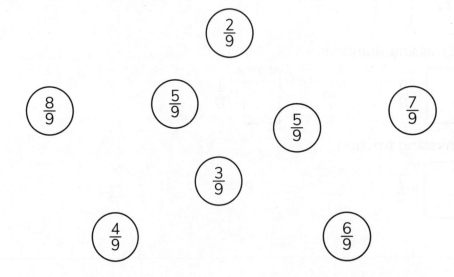

9 Find different ways to solve this calculation.

$$\frac{\square}{\square} + \frac{\square}{\square} = \frac{4}{3}$$

_____

_____

10 Write the missing numbers.

a $\frac{7}{9} - \boxed{} = \frac{2}{9}$

b $\boxed{} - \frac{2}{7} = \frac{3}{7}$

Challenge

11 Find the missing numbers.

$\frac{2}{7} + \boxed{} = \frac{6}{7}$

$\frac{3}{4} + \boxed{} = \frac{5}{4}$

$\frac{5}{9} + \boxed{} = \frac{10}{9}$

$\boxed{} + \frac{2}{3} = \frac{5}{3}$

$\boxed{} + \frac{6}{8} = \frac{7}{8}$

$\boxed{} + \frac{3}{6} = \frac{7}{6}$

$\frac{8}{9} - \boxed{} = \frac{4}{9}$

$\frac{6}{9} - \boxed{} = \frac{3}{9}$

$\frac{11}{12} - \boxed{} = \frac{2}{12}$

$\boxed{} - \frac{2}{5} = \frac{1}{5}$

$\boxed{} - \frac{5}{7} = \frac{1}{7}$

$\boxed{} - \frac{4}{9} = \frac{3}{9}$

12 Find different ways to solve this calculation.

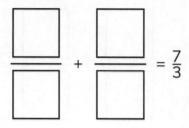

$$\frac{\square}{\square} + \frac{\square}{\square} = \frac{7}{3}$$

13 a Write two fractions that have a sum of $\frac{7}{8}$.

b Write two fractions that have a difference of $\frac{3}{8}$.

14 Find the missing fraction.

$$\boxed{} - \frac{2}{9} = \frac{3}{9} + \frac{2}{9} + \frac{1}{9}$$

15 In the diagram the fraction in each box is the sum of the two fractions below it. Write the missing fractions.

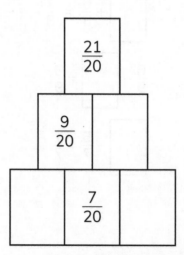

14 ▶ Area and perimeter

> 14.1 Estimating and measuring area and perimeter

Worked example 1

Measure and calculate the perimeter of this shape.

> area   perimeter

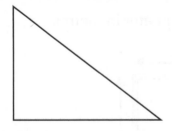

Place your ruler carefully along each side of the shape and record the length of each side. Remember the units.

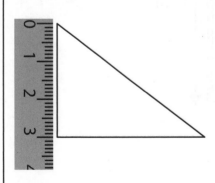 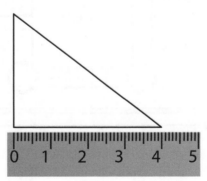 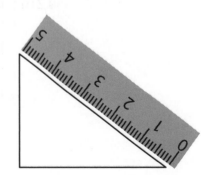

The sides are 3 cm, 4 cm and 5 cm.

3 + 4 + 5 = 12   Add together the side lengths to find the perimeter.

Answer: The perimeter of the shape is 12 cm.

Exercise 14.1

Focus

1   Add the lengths of the lines to find the perimeter of the rectangle.

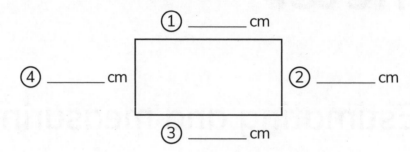

① _____ cm

④ _____ cm   ② _____ cm

③ _____ cm

Line 1 = _____ cm   Line 2 = _____ cm

Line 3 = _____ cm   Line 4 = _____ cm

Perimeter = _____ cm

2   Add up the lengths of the castle walls to find the perimeter in metres.

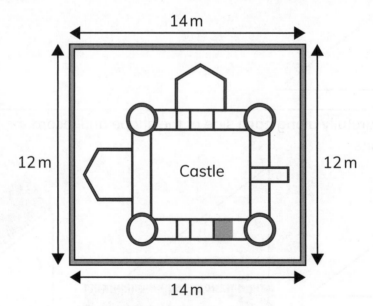

14 m

12 m   Castle   12 m

14 m

3 Draw and shade three more different shapes on this centimetre square paper that have an area of 8 cm².

1																
2																
3	6															
4	7															
5	8															

4 Number the squares that have over half shaded to estimate the area. Write the area in cm².

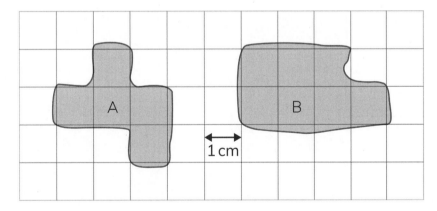

a Area of shape A = _____

b Area of shape B = _____

c Add the areas together to estimate the total shaded area.

Total area is _____

Practice

5   Measure and record the perimeter of each rectangle.
    Remember to use the correct units.

a

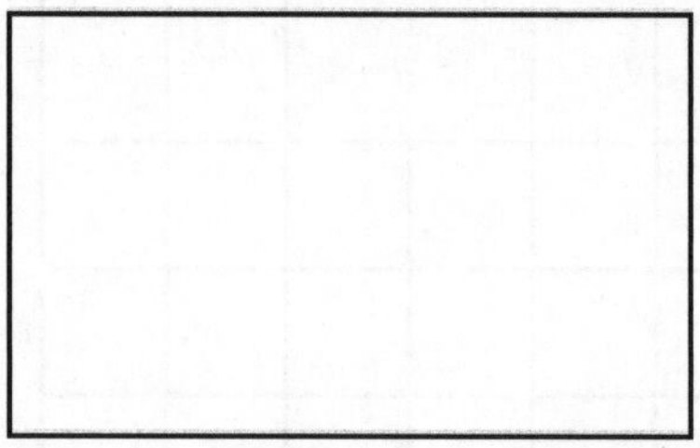

_____

b

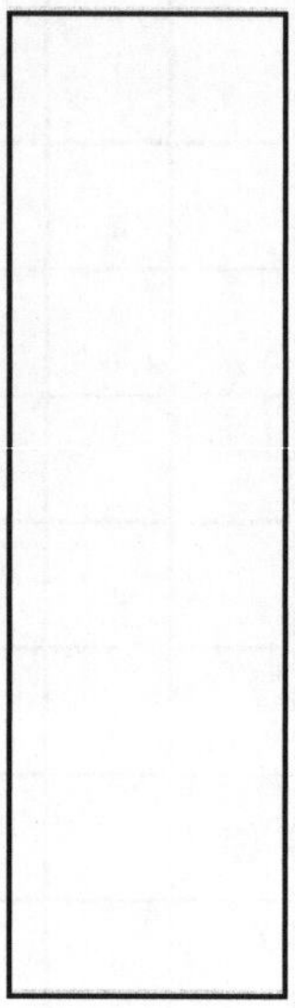

_____

c

_____

6   Add up the lengths around the park to find out how long the perimeter fence is.
    Remember to use the correct units.

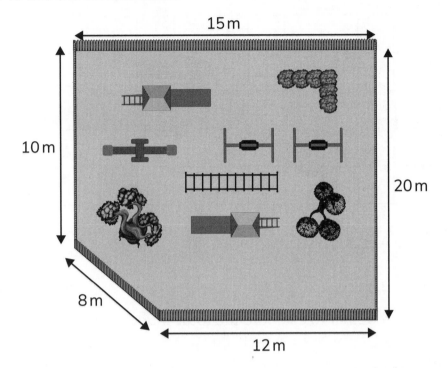

The perimeter fence is _____

 7   Divide this shape into four sections so that each section has an area of 9 cm².

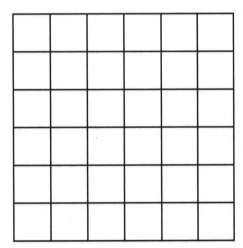

8 Number the squares that are over half shaded to estimate the area.
   Write the area in the correct square units.

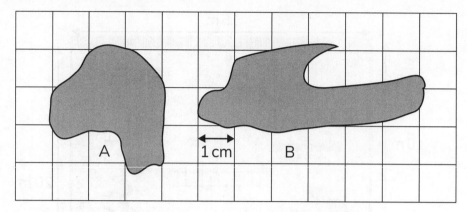

a   Area of shape A is _____

b   Area of shape B is _____

c   Add the areas together to estimate the total shaded area.

    Total area is _____

Challenge

9 Measure and record the perimeter of this shape in millimetres.

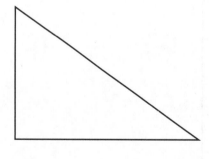

_____

10 Estimate the total shaded area.

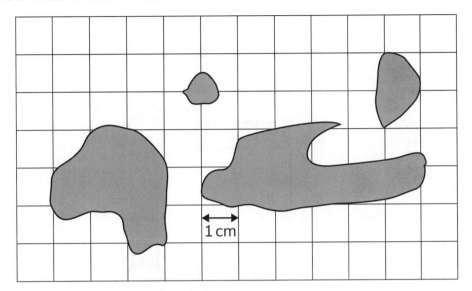

The total shaded area is approximately _____

 11 On this centimetre square paper draw and shade four different shapes with curved sides that each have an estimated area of 6 cm².

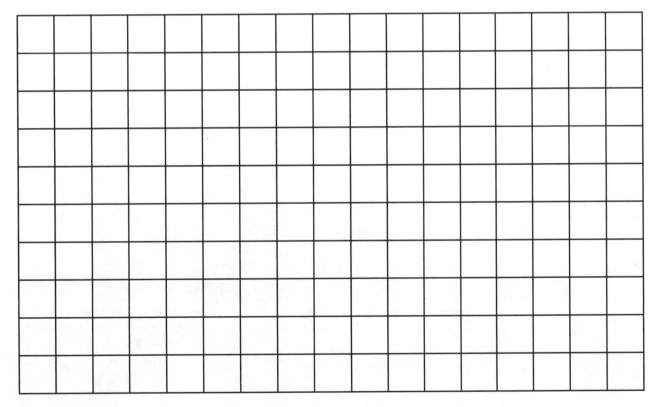

12 What is the perimeter of the castle wall?

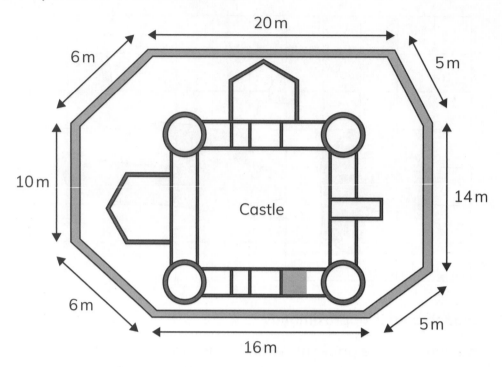

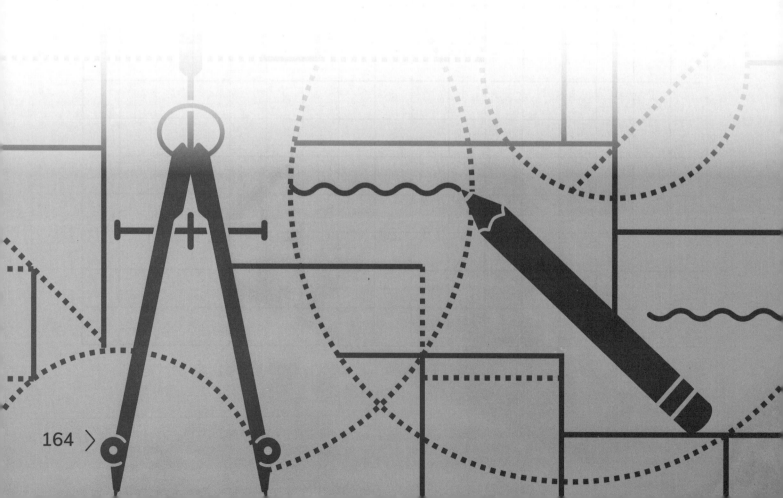

› 14.2 Area and perimeter of rectangles

Worked example 2

Find the area of this rectangle.

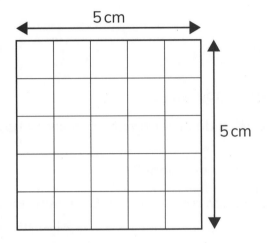

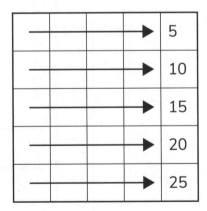

Count the squares to find the area. This rectangle has 5 squares in each row so you can count the squares in 5s.

Answer: The area is 25 cm².

Exercise 14.2

Focus

1   Join the dots carefully with a ruler.

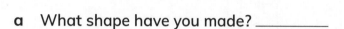

    a What shape have you made? _____

    b Measure and label each side in centimetres to show how long it is.

    c What is the perimeter of your shape? _____

2 **a** How many squares in each row of this rectangle?

        b Count in 3s to find out how many squares altogether.

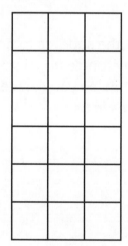

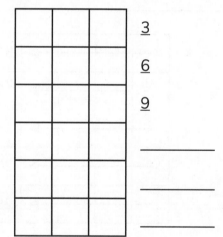

3

6

9

_____

_____

_____

_____ squares

    c Measure one side of a square in the rectangle.

        1 square is _____ wide.

    d Circle the correct area for the rectangle.

$$18\,mm^2 \qquad 18\,cm^2 \qquad 18\,m^2 \qquad 18\,km^2$$

3   Look at this rectangle.

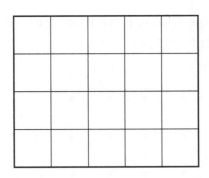

a   How many squares in each row? _____

b   Use a ruler to measure the length of the rectangle.

The rectangle is _____ cm long.

c   How many squares are there in each column? _____

d   Use a ruler to measure the width of the rectangle.

The rectangle is _____ wide.

e   Use these words to complete the sentence.

| length | row | squares |

The _____ of the rectangle is the same as the number of _____

in a _____ .

Practice

4   In this space draw a rectangle that is 8 cm long and 5 cm wide.
    The distance between the dots is 1cm.

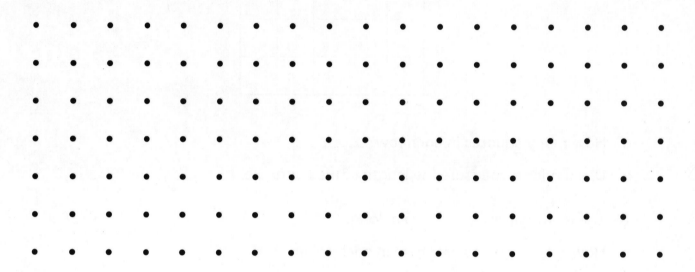

What is the perimeter of your rectangle? _____

5   a   How many squares are there in each row of this rectangle?

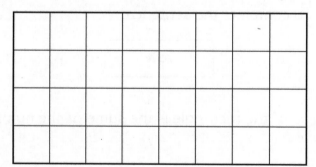

_____ squares

b   Circle the correct area for the whole rectangle.

8 cm²   36 mm²   28 cm²   32 m²   32 cm²   24 km²

6   Complete the sentences to describe the rectangle.

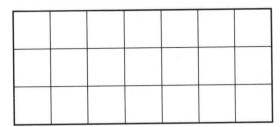

There are _____ squares in each row and _____ squares in each column.

The rectangle is _____ cm long and _____ wide.

_____ rows of _____ makes _____ squares altogether.

The area of the rectangle is _____ multiplied by _____ .

The area of the rectangle is _____ cm².

7   Calculate the area and perimeter of these rectangles using the measurements shown.
    Remember to record the units.

a

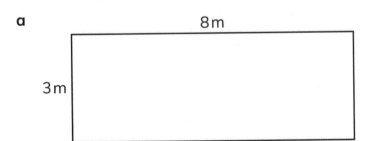

    Area is _____   Perimeter is _____

b

    Area is _____   Perimeter is _____

c

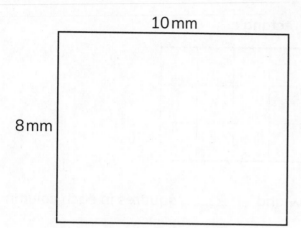

Area is _____   Perimeter is _____

d

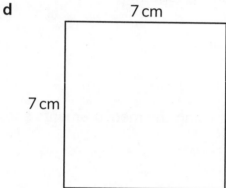

Area is _____   Perimeter is _____

Challenge

8   Draw a rectangle that is 5 cm long and 4 cm wide. Use a ruler.

Find the perimeter and area.

Perimeter = _____   Area = _____

9 Without measuring, work out the missing lengths from these rectangles.
   Write in the missing lengths and work out the perimeter of each rectangle.

a

3 m

1 m

_____

_____

Perimeter is _____

b

_____

9 km

_____

6 km

Perimeter is _____

c

72 mm

_____   6 mm

_____

Perimeter is _____

10 Explain in words how you can use the measurements for the length and
   width of a rectangle to calculate its area.

_____

_____

_____

11 Calculate the area of these rectangles using the measurements shown.

a

5 km

12 km

Area is _____

b

9 mm

11 mm

Area is _____

c

8 cm

8 cm

Area is _____

d

2 m

$3\frac{1}{2}$ m

Area is _____

15 > Special numbers

> 15.1 Ordering and comparing numbers

negative number   order

Worked example 1

Write these temperatures in order starting with the lowest temperature.

−14 °C   4 °C   14 °C   −1 °C   0 °C   −8 °C

Think about where the numbers go on a number line.

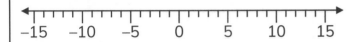

Order the negative numbers first, then zero, then the positive numbers.

Negative numbers are always smaller than positive numbers.

Answer: −14 °C, −8 °C, −1 °C, 0 °C, 4 °C, 14 °C

Exercise 15.1

Focus

1   Write each set of temperatures in order starting with the coldest temperature.
Use the number line to help you. Remember that as you move to the right (→)
numbers get larger.

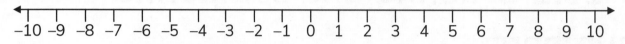

-10 -9 -8 -7 -6 -5 -4 -3 -2 -1 0 1 2 3 4 5 6 7 8 9 10

a   0 °C   −9 °C   3 °C   −2 °C

_____

b   3 °C   −4 °C   7 °C   −8 °C

_____

c   −2 °C   2 °C   7 °C   −10 °C

_____

2   a   Write these numbers in order starting with the smallest.

−5   5   10   −15   0   −10

_____

b   Describe the number pattern you have made.

_____

c   If you continue the pattern, will you write 71?
How do you know without writing all the numbers?

_____

_____

3   Which is larger −4 or −1?
Write your answer using one of the symbols > or <

_____

> **Tip**
>
> Use the number
> line in question 1
> to help you.

4 If $-7 <$ ☐ < -4 what whole number could ☐ be?

Practice

5 Write each set of temperatures in order, starting with the coldest temperature.

   a $-4\,°C$ $1\,°C$ $-8\,°C$ $-2\,°C$ $3\,°C$

   b $-2\,°C$ $4\,°C$ $-7\,°C$ $-13\,°C$ $13\,°C$

   c $6\,°C$ $-6\,°C$ $0\,°C$ $-7\,°C$ $-4\,°C$

6 Compare each pair of numbers and fill in the boxes using the symbols > or <

                6 ☐ -17 -16 ☐ -13 0 ☐ -2

 7 Write each number in one box to make these statements correct.

       -13 -4 7 -17 5 12 -3

   Find a different possible answer to the problem.

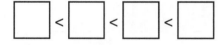

 8 Circle all the numbers that are greater than -6 but less than 4.

              -8 -10 5 -4 0

Challenge

9   Hassan makes a sequence of numbers. His rule is to add the
    same amount each time. Write the missing numbers.

| −22 | | | | 6 |

Use your numbers to make this statement correct.

☐ > ☐ > ☐ > ☐ > ☐

10 The table shows the average temperatures in some cities in January.

City	Temperature (°C)
Bejing, China	−3
Budapest, Hungary	1
Delhi, India	14
Istanbul, Turkey	5
Karachi, Pakistan	18
Moscow, Russia	−8
Ulaanbaatar, Mongolia	−20

a   Which is the coldest place?

_____

b   Which is the warmest place?

_____

c   Put the temperatures in order starting with the coldest.

_____

11 Compare each pair of numbers using the symbols > or < .

−3 ☐ −4   −19 ☐ 11   0 ☐ −1

12 A sequence starts at 50, and 8 is subtracted each time.

50   42   34 . . .

If the sequence continues in the same way, what are the first two numbers less than zero?

⟩ 15.2 Working with special numbers

Worked example 2	even factor multiple odd square number

Here are four labels.

multiple of 5		not a multiple of 5		odd		even

Write the labels on the sorting diagram.

	30
	       50
		5
		       35

	18
	       6
		7
		       11

	even	**odd**

	30
	       50
		5
		       35

	18
	       6
		7
		       11

Work systematically.

Look at **all** the numbers in the first column and place the label.

All the numbers in the first column are even.

Then look at **all** the numbers in the second column.

All the numbers in the second column are odd.

Repeat for each row.

Continued

Answer:

	even	odd
multiple of 5	30　　50	5　　35
not a multiple of 5	18　　6	7　　11

Exercise 15.2

Focus

1 Colour all the odd numbers. What is the hidden number?

416	636	50	32	412	806	154
232	135	220	53	861	657	72
198	687	8	100	654	423	98
110	909	68	851	595	677	86
404	45	676	53	358	730	590
206	701	294	825	117	5	358
682	566	742	174	552	340	246

You could use squared paper to make similar puzzles for your friends to try.

2 Look at the number grid.

Circle all the multiples of 7.

61	62	63	64	65	66
67	68	69	70	71	72
73	74	75	76	77	78

3 ☐ stands for a missing number.

Write the missing number and missing words in these number sentences.

3 and 7 are _____ of ☐ because 3 × 7 = ☐

☐ is a _____ of 3 and 7 because ☐ ÷ 3 = 7 and ☐ ÷ 7 = 3

 4 Put a cross (X) through the number that is in the wrong place.
Write it in the correct place.

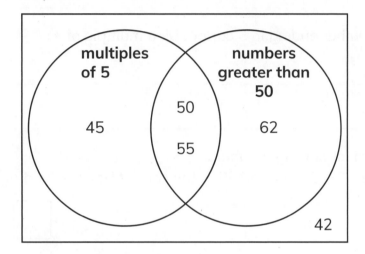

5 Write all the factor pairs for 24.

☐ × ☐ = 24   ☐ × ☐ = 24

☐ × ☐ = 24   ☐ × ☐ = 24

 6 Kojo says, 'Nine is a square number.'
Is Kojo correct? Explain how you know.

_____

_____

Practice

7   Kofi is thinking of a number.

  • It is a multiple of 3.

  • It is a multiple of 5.

  • It is an odd number.

  • It is between 20 and 60.

  What is Kofi's number?

_____

 8   Explain why a number ending in 5 cannot be a multiple of 4.

_____

_____

9   Here is a diagram for sorting numbers.
  Write the numbers 24, 25, 64 and 65 in the correct box on the diagram.

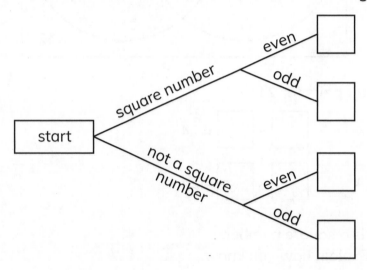

10 a   Write all the factors of 20.

_____

  b   Write all the multiples of 20 that are less than 100.

_____

11 Use four different square numbers to make these calculations correct.

$\boxed{} + \boxed{} = 5$ $\qquad$ $\boxed{} + \boxed{} = 25$

Challenge

12 Write the 2-digit odd number that is a multiple of 7.

4	

What is special about this number?

_____

13 Here are four digit cards.

3		4		5		6

Use each of these cards to make a total that is a multiple of 6.
Each card can only be used once.

		and		

14 Look at these numbers and complete the sentences.

8		12		25		40

a 8 is the odd one out because _____

_____

b 12 is the odd one out because _____

_____

c 25 is the odd one out because _____

_____

d 40 is the odd one out because _____

_____

15 Use this tree diagram to sort a set of whole numbers. You could use 18, −24, 27, 19, 14, −21, −5, −14, or choose numbers of your own.

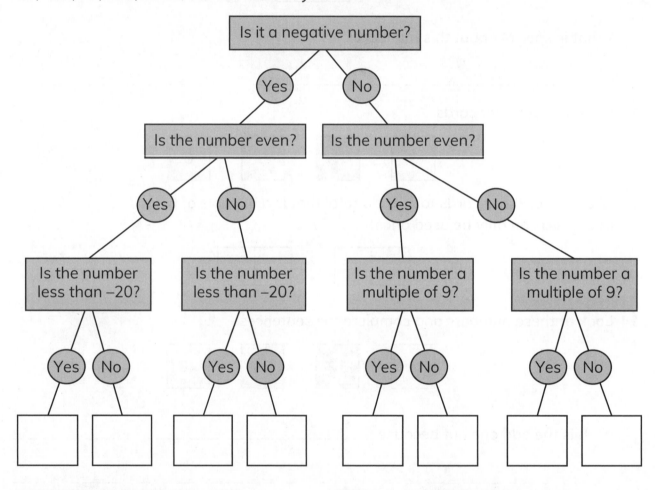

⟩ 15.3 Tests of divisibility

Worked example 3

Use all the digits 8, 0, 9 and 5 to make the smallest
4-digit number that is divisible by both 2 and 5.

divisibility rule   divisible

A number that is divisible by both 2 and 5 must be divisible by 10.

The number will have 0 in the ones place.

Arrange the other digits to make the smallest possible number.

Answer: 5890

Exercise 15.3

Focus

1   Circle all the numbers that are divisible by 2.

232   234   243   223   251   215

2   Write these numbers in the Venn diagram.

302   25   203   400   205   52   502

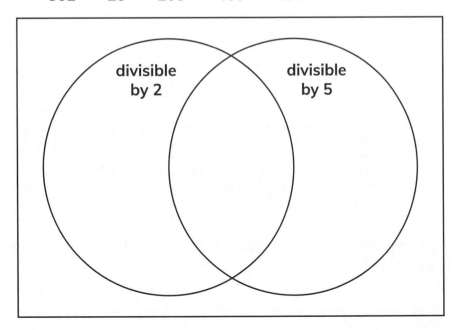

3   Draw a line to complete the divisibility rules.

Divisible by 2	ones digit is 0 or 5
Divisible by 5	tens and ones digits are 0
Divisible by 10	ones digit is 0, 2, 4, 6 or 8
Divisible by 100	ones digit is 0

Practice

4   Use one of these numbers to complete each sentence.

2   5   10   100

a   A number is divisible by _____ if the ones digit is 0, 2, 4, 6 or 8.

b   A number is divisible by _____ if the ones digit is 0.

5   Write these numbers in the table.

25   500   310   1000   105   690

Divisible by 5	Divisible by 5 and 10	Divisible by 5, 10 and 100

6   Colour every number that is divisible by 2, 5 or 10.

1	70	20	80	3	13	61	17	43	52	54	90	31
27	4	63	32	69	39	44	19	29	75	9	14	59
67	62	46	10	53	22	70	25	7	12	28	55	73
63	8	17	34	29	77	32	71	43	59	49	62	79
41	30	38	34	73	33	51	51	69	53	57	105	87

What is the answer to the secret calculation that appears when you have coloured the numbers?

Challenge

7   Alex says, 'The number fifteen thousand five hundred and fifty-three is divisible by 5.'
    Is he correct? Explain how you know.

    _____

    _____

8   Which of these numbers is divisible by 5 but not by 2 or 10?

                         250   205   502   520

    How do you know?

    _____

    _____

    Write down two more numbers that are divisible by 5 but not by 2 or 10.

    _____

9   Here is a set of numbers.

                    20, 50, 75, 300, 350, 600, 650, 675

    a   Write all the numbers that are divisible by 100.

        _____

    b   Write all the numbers that are divisible by 50.

        _____

    c   Write all the numbers that are divisible by 25.

        _____

10 What is the smallest number that can be added to 333 to make it divisible by 25?

    _____

Data display and interpretation

＞ 16.1 Displaying and interpreting data

Worked example 1

Display the data in this frequency table using a bar chart.

Frequency table showing how many pets each person has

Number of pets	Number of people
0	10
1	13
2	7
3	4
4	2

> **Tip**
>
> Always use a ruler and work neatly so that the bar chart will be easy to read and interpret.

Answer:

Choose a scale for the vertical axis. The highest number in the data is 13, so the axis must go up to at least 13. The data will be clearest if it is labelled in 1s or 2s.

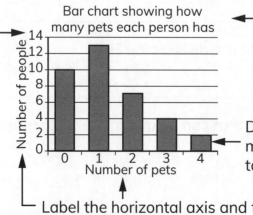

Bar chart showing how many pets each person has

Add a title. The title explains what the data is about.

Draw bars, using the scale to match the data in the table to the data in the bar chart.

Label the horizontal axis and the vertical axis. The headings in the table can be used to label the axes.

bar chart   Carroll diagram   pictogram   Venn diagram

Exercise 16.1

Focus

1   Label each diagram, chart or graph with its name.

| pictogram | Venn diagram | Carroll diagram |
| bar chart | dot plot | frequency table |

a

Sweet colour	Number in the packet
red	✕●✕ ✕●✕ ✕●✕
yellow	✕●✕ ✕◗
green	✕●✕ ✕●✕ ✕◗

key: ✕●✕ = 2 sweets

_____

b

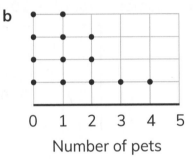

0   1   2   3   4   5

Number of pets

_____

c

	Even	Not even
Multiple of 10		
Not a multiple of 10		

_____

d

Coin	Number of coins
5 cents	4
10 cents	1
25 cents	2
50 cents	1

_____

2 Circle the chart or diagram you should use for displaying each set of data.
   Explain why you would use that chart or diagram.

   a Sorting the colour and name of a set of shapes. I would use a

      Pictogram / Carroll diagram because _____ .

      _____

   b Showing how many people voted for different songs. I would use a

      Venn diagram / Bar chart because _____ .

      _____

3 Sort the numbers from 1 to 20 into this Venn diagram.

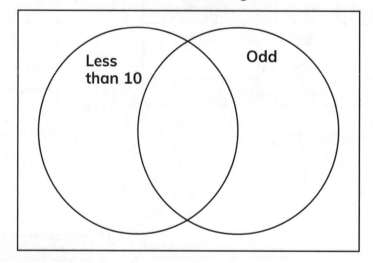

4 Choose your own categories to sort shapes in this Carroll diagram.

   Choose a colour

   Choose a shape
   name

   _____   not _____

   _____

   not _____

   Draw and colour two shapes in each section to match the properties you
   have chosen.

5   Display the data in this frequency table using a bar chart.
    Frequency table showing how many pets each person has

Number of pets	Number of people
0	20
1	14
2	9
3	3
4	1

You can use Worked example 1 to help you.

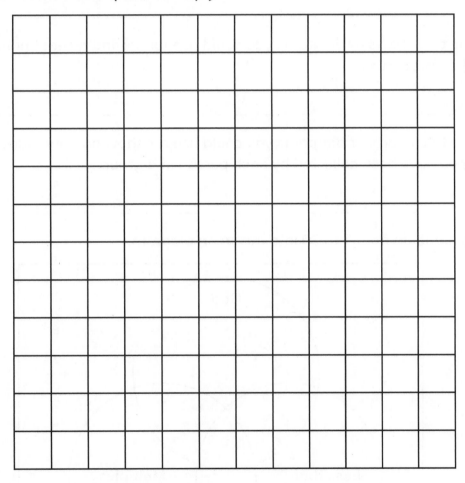

a   How many people have two pets? _____

b   How many people have more than two pets? _____

Practice

6 Name the type of diagram, chart or graph.

a

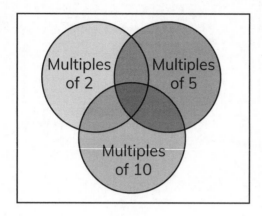

b

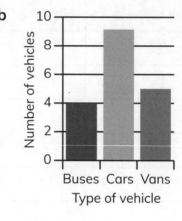

_____   _____

7 a Name two charts or diagrams you could use for sorting a set of numbers
by their properties.

_____

b Name two charts or diagrams you could use for showing how many
stamps have been collected by each person in a group.

_____

8 Sort the numbers from 1 to 30 into this Venn diagram.

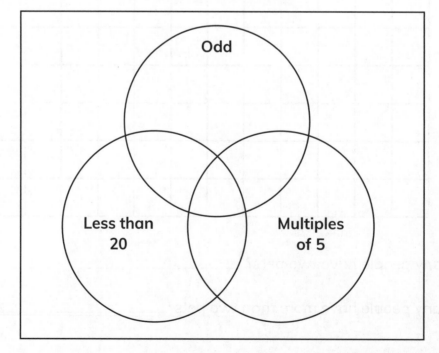

9 Four girls are sorted into this Carroll diagram.

	Curly hair	Not curly hair
Wearing glasses	Amira	Bibi
Not wearing glasses	Clara	Delia

Draw a picture of Clara.

10 You are going to investigate the length of the names of people you know.

Write 30 first names of people that you know. You can write one name in each box.

Mark the length of each name on this tally chart and find the frequency for each group of lengths.

Number of letters in the name	Tally	Frequency
1 to 3		
4 to 6		
7 to 9		
10 or more		

Choose a type of graph or chart to represent your data.

What type of graph or chart will you use? _____

Why will you use that type of graph or chart? _____

_____.

Use this space to draw your graph or chart.

Write two sentences to describe what you have found out about the length of first names of people you know.

1 _____.

2 _____.

11 Daisy counted the birds she saw outside her window for one hour each day for five days. The bar chart shows her results.

Number of birds Daisy saw each day

Kwame counted the birds he saw outside his window for one hour each day for five days. This frequency table shows his results.

Number of birds Kwame saw on each day

Day	Number of birds
1	10
2	7
3	7
4	4
5	3

Draw a bar chart of the birds Kwame saw.
Use the same scale as the bar chart for the birds that Daisy saw.

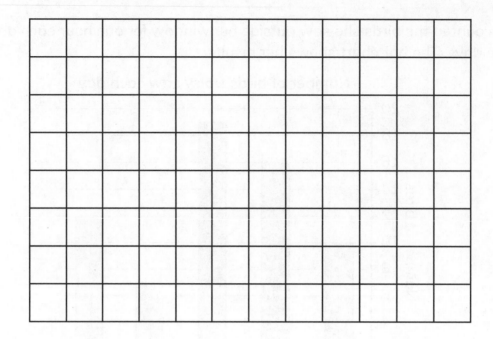

a   Describe one similarity between the two sets of data.

_____

b   Describe one difference between the two sets of data.

_____

c   Explain a possible reason for the differences in the data.

_____

_____

Challenge

12 a   Explain what a Carroll diagram might be used for.

_____

b   Explain what a pictogram might be used for.

_____

13 a Circle the numbers that are in the wrong place in this Venn diagram.

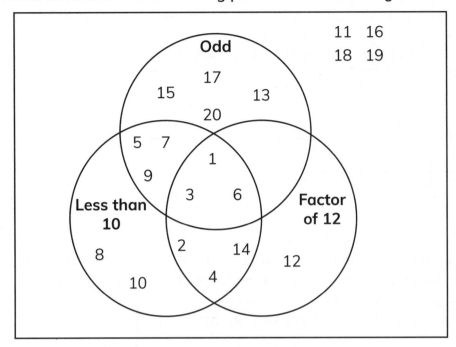

b Explain why one of the sections has no numbers in it.

_____

_____

14 Choose your own categories to sort 3D shapes in this Carroll diagram.

Write the names of at least one 3D shape in each section to match the properties you have chosen. If you cannot find a shape to match a section you will need to change your headings.

15 Anna timed how long it took her to get to school each day for five days.
This frequency table shows how long it took Anna to get to school each day.

Day	Number of minutes to get to school
1	25
2	17
3	19
4	23
5	28

Carlos timed how long it took him to get to school for the same five days.
This frequency table shows how long it took Carlos to get to school.

Day	Number of minutes to get to school
1	11
2	9
3	11
4	15
5	18

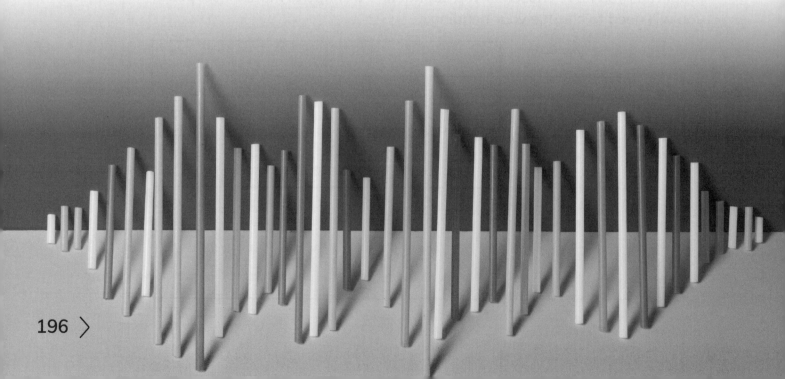

Draw two bar charts on the grid provided to display the time it took Anna and Carlos to get to school.

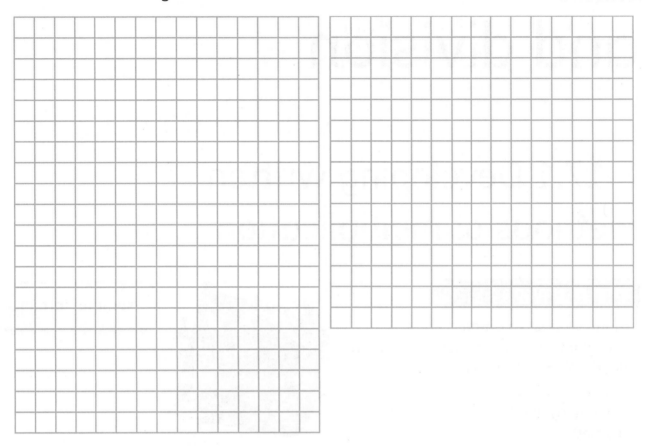

a   Why is it useful to use the same scale for both bar charts?

_____

b   Describe one similarity between the two sets of data.

_____

c   Describe one difference between the two sets of data.

_____

d   Explain a possible reason for the differences in the data.

_____

_____

17 ▶ Multiplication and division

› 17.1 Developing written methods of multiplication

> **Worked example 1**
>
> Ingrid works in a garden centre.
> She plants 4 seeds in each cell in a tray.
> Each tray has 270 cells.
> She fills every cell.
> How many seeds does Ingrid plant altogether?

estimate   product

Ingrid works in a garden centre.	Read the problem carefully.
She plants <u>4 seeds in each cell in a tray</u>.	Underline the important information.
Each tray has <u>270 cells</u>.	
She <u>fills every cell</u>.	
You need to work out 270 × 4	Decide what calculation to do.
Estimate:	Estimate the answer.
200 × 4 = 800	
300 × 4 = 1200	
So the answer will be between 800 and 1200	

Continued

	2	7	0
	×		4
1	0	8	0
	2		

Answer: 270 × 4 = 1080 seeds

Calculate 270 × 4

Use the estimate to check that the answer is reasonable.

Exercise 17.1

Focus

1   Leanne collects 2 comics each month for a year.

How many comics does she collect in a year?

Tip

In this exercise, remember to estimate before you calculate.

Tip

Remember there are 12 months in a year.

2 Mr Singh has 13 boxes of tinned tomatoes.
Each box contains 6 tins of tomatoes.
How many tins of tomatoes has Mr Singh got altogether?
Show your working.

3 Explain what is wrong in this calculation. Work out the correct answer.

correct answer

		4	7
	×		6
2	4	4	2

		4	7
	×		6

4 Orla estimates the answer to 298 × 8 to be 2400.
Is this a good estimate? Explain your answer.

5 Fatima reads 48 pages of a book.
Parveen reads four times as many pages as Fatima.
How many more pages did Parveen read than Fatima?
Show your working.

Tip

Start by working out
how many pages
Parveen reads.

Practice

6 Find the product of 58 and 5.

_____

 7 Multiply the numbers in two circles to give the number in the square between them.
Fill in the missing numbers.

a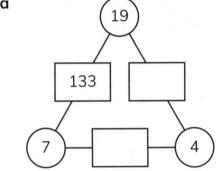

b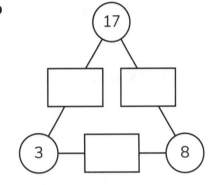

 8 Erik and Ollie complete the same multiplication.

Erik

	100s	10s	1s
	3	4	5
	×		4
1	2	8	0
		1	2

Ollie

	100s	10s	1s
	3	4	5
	×		4
1	3	8	0
		1	2

Who has the correct answer? _____

What mistake has the other boy made?

_____

_____

9 Milly buys 4 packets of red balloons.

Paula buys 2 packets of blue balloons.

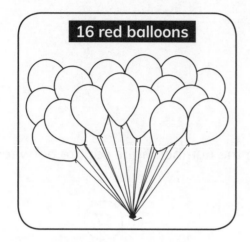

Milly says, 'I have four times as many balloons as Paula.'
Is Milly correct? Explain your answer.

_____

_____

10 Here are some digit cards.

1   3   5   7   0

Use three of these cards to make this calculation correct.

☐☐ × ☐ = 150

Challenge

11 Use the digits 1, 2, 8 and 9 to make the multiplication that has the greatest product.

☐☐☐ × ☐ =

12 Find the mistake in this calculation.

correct calculation

	7	4	1
	×		5
3	5	2	5

	7	4	1
	×		5

Explain what is wrong and write the correct calculation.

_____

_____

 13 Here are four digit cards.

 2   4   6   8

Use three of these cards to make this calculation correct.

☐ 0 × ☐ = 3 ☐ 0

14 Write the **same** digit in each box to make the calculation correct.

4	☐	6
	×	☐
3	3	3	2

 15 Magda says, 'If you add three consecutive numbers, the sum is three times the middle number.'

Is she right?

Give three examples of 2-digit numbers to justify your answer.

_____

_____

> 17.2 Developing written methods of division

Worked example 2

A group of friends earn $72 by washing cars.
They share the money equally.
They each earn $6.
How many friends are in the group?

A group of friends earn $72 by washing cars.	Read the problem carefully.
They share the money equally.	Underline the important information.
They each earn $6.	
You need to work out 72 ÷ 6	Decide which calculation to do.
Estimate:	
60 ÷ 6 = 10	Estimate the answer.
120 ÷ 6 = 20	
So the answer will be between 10 and 20	
$$\begin{array}{r} 12 \\ 6\overline{)7^12} \end{array}$$	Calculate 72 ÷ 6
	Use the estimate to check that the answer is reasonable.

Answer: 72 ÷ 6 = 12 friends

dividend   divisor   quotient   remainder

Exercise 17.2

Focus

Tip

Remember to estimate before you calculate.

1   Write the number that is half of 58.

_____

2   Yuri has 96 triangular tiles.

He uses them to make hexagons like this.

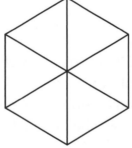

How many hexagons can Yuri make?

_____

3   Pencils cost 9 cents each. Myrtle has 52 cents.

9 cents each

Tip

You need to find the remainder.

How many pencils can she buy?
How much money will Myrtle have left?

_____   _____

 4   Conrad has 50 eggs.
A box holds 6 eggs.
Conrad says he needs 8 boxes.
Is Conrad correct? Explain your answer.

_____

_____

5 Apples are sold in trays of 4.
   Tara has 58 apples to pack in trays.

   How many trays does Tara need to pack all her apples?

   _____

Practice

6 Petra wants to put 62 photos in an album.
   A full page holds 4 photos.
   She fills as many whole pages as possible.
   How many photos does she have left over?

   _____

 7 Which pairs of numbers can be written in the boxes?

   24 ÷ ☐ = ☐

 8 Put each calculation in the correct box.

25 ÷ 4 = 5	70 ÷ 7 = 10	76 ÷ 9 = 8
63 ÷ 7 = 9	84 ÷ 8 = 11	29 ÷ 3 = 9
76 ÷ 9 = 8	63 ÷ 9 = 7	45 ÷ 5 = 9

True	False

9 There are 160 students in Year 4.
A teacher orders 6 boxes of pens. Each box contains 24 pens.
Has the teacher ordered enough pens to give one to each student?
Explain your answer.

_____

_____

10 Find the missing digit.

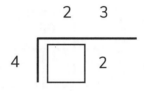

$$
\begin{array}{r}
23 \\
4\,\overline{\smash{)}\,\square\,2}
\end{array}
$$

Challenge

11 Which pairs of numbers could be written in the boxes?

$48 \div \boxed{} = \boxed{}$

_____

_____

12 Find the odd one out. Explain your answer.

$48 \div 4$ $96 \div 8$ $84 \div 7$ $75 \div 5$ $72 \div 6$

_____

_____

_____

13 Use <, > or = to complete these statements.

$$96 \div 4 \bigcirc 96 \div 3$$

$$69 \div 3 \bigcirc 96 \div 3$$

$$91 \div 7 \bigcirc 84 \div 3$$

14 In the diagram, the number in each box is the product of the two numbers below it. Write the missing numbers.

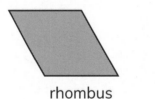

15 Magda has two different types of tile.

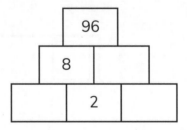

rhombus   triangle

She uses 4 triangles and 2 rhombuses to make a 'fish'.

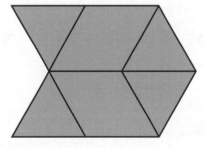

Magda uses 56 triangles to make some fish.
How many rhombuses does she use?

18 ▸ Position, direction and movement

› 18.1 Position and movement

Worked example 1

Worked example 1

What is the position of X on the grid?

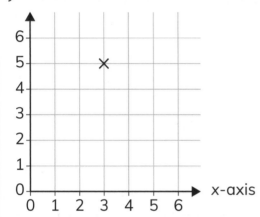

You can use coordinates to describe a position on a grid.

First use the x-axis to find the horizontal position of the X.

The X is 3 squares across.

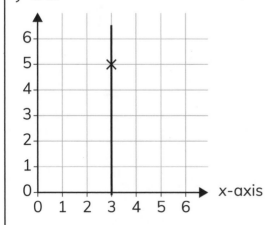

Continued

y-axis

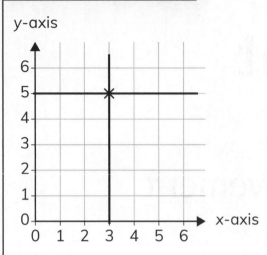

x-axis

Next use the y-axis to find the vertical position of the X.

The X is 5 squares up.

y-axis

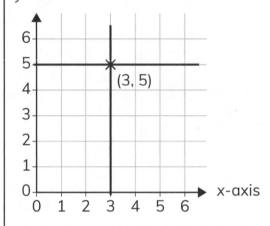

x-axis

Write the number as coordinates: (horizontal position, vertical position).

The point where the lines cross has coordinates (3, 5).

Answer: The position of X on the grid is (3, 5)

compass coordinates quadrant

Exercise 18.1

Focus

1   Complete the compass directions.

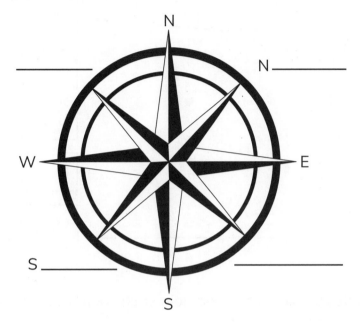

2   Describe the direction of the path from flag to flag using compass directions.

1 _____

2 _____

3 _____

4 _____

5 _____

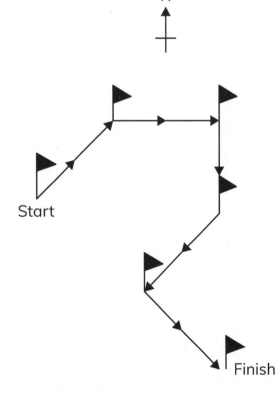

3 Draw an arrow from the coordinates to the cross in the correct position.
Remember, the first number (x) is how far horizontally,
the second number (y) is how far vertically. (↔, ↕)

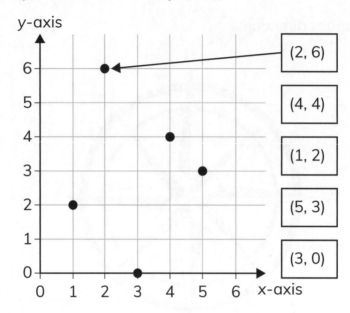

4 Mark the coordinates below on the grid. Join each coordinate to the next
and then join the last coordinate to the first to make a polygon.

2 across and 3 up (2, 3)

4 across and 1 up (4, 1)

5 across and 2 up (5, 2)

3 across and 6 up (3, 6)

2 across and 5 up (2, 5)

What is the name of the polygon you
have made?

_____

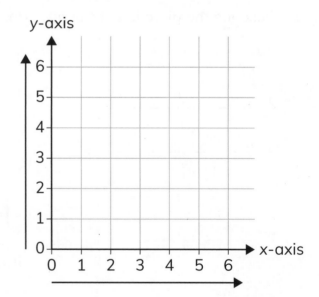

Practice

5 This is a map of the town where Halim lives.

Map of Halim's Town

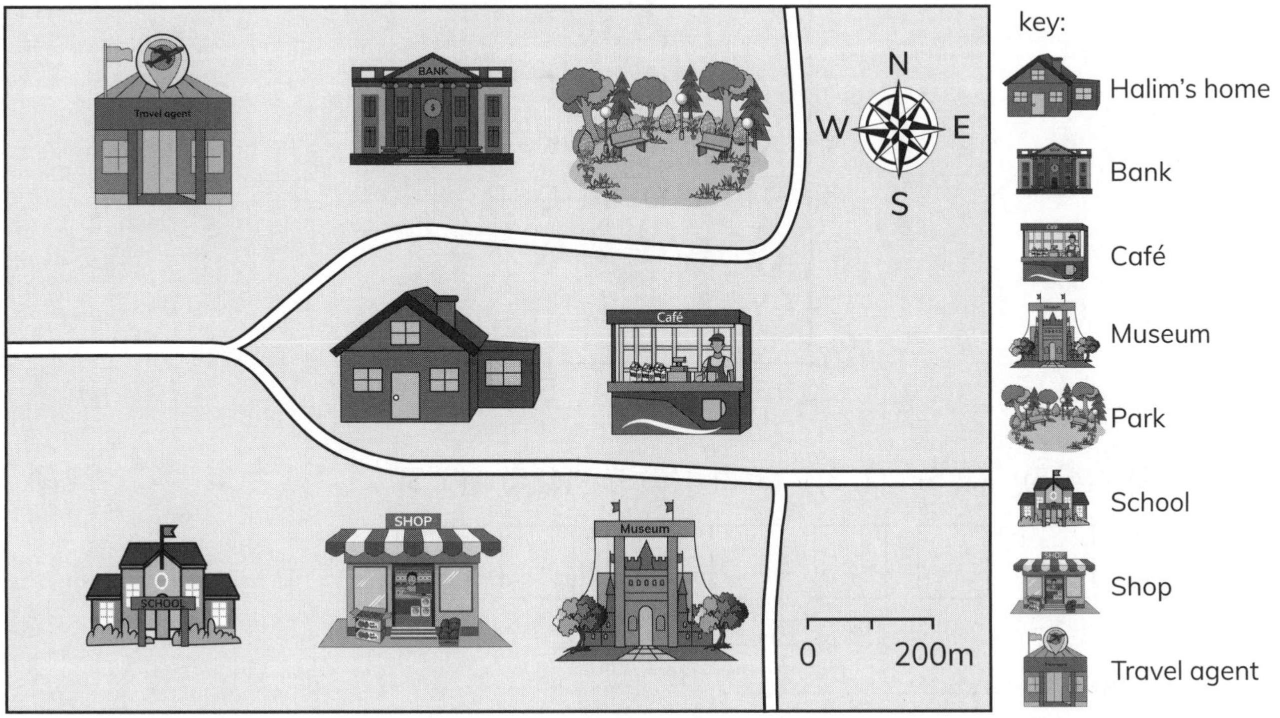

Travel agent
BANK
Café
SHOP
Museum
SCHOOL
N
W
E
S
0
200m
key:
Halim's home
Bank
Café
Museum
Park
School
Shop
Travel agent

a What compass direction should Halim follow to get from his home to:

i the shop? ________________

ii the school? ________________

iii the park? ________________

b What is the compass direction from the café to the bank?

____

c What is the compass direction from the bank to the café?

____

6 Write the letter that is at each of these coordinates.
Rearrange the letters to reveal a word about the coordinates.

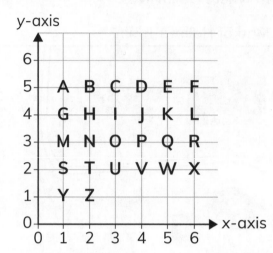

(2, 2) (4, 5) (1, 5) (2, 3) (3, 2) (6, 3) (1, 5) (5, 3)

⬜ ⬜ ⬜ ⬜ ⬜ ⬜ ⬜ ⬜

The word is: _____

7 a Mark the coordinates listed on the grid.

A (3, 4)   B (0, 6)   C (3, 6)   D (0, 4)

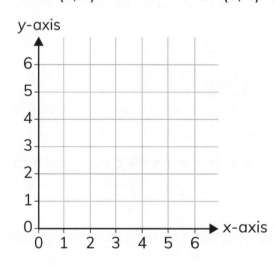

Join the four coordinates in order with a ruler. Join the last coordinate to the first.

b What polygon is made? _____

Challenge

8   Complete this compass with the compass directions, and write the number
    of degrees turn that each direction is from North.

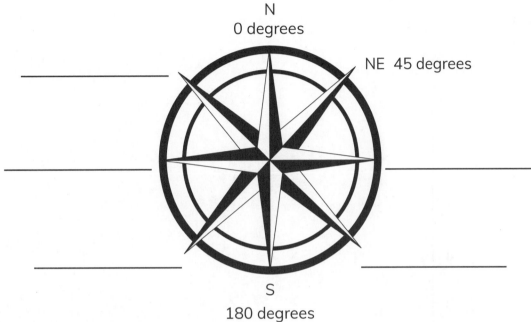

9   Label the coordinates of each ●.

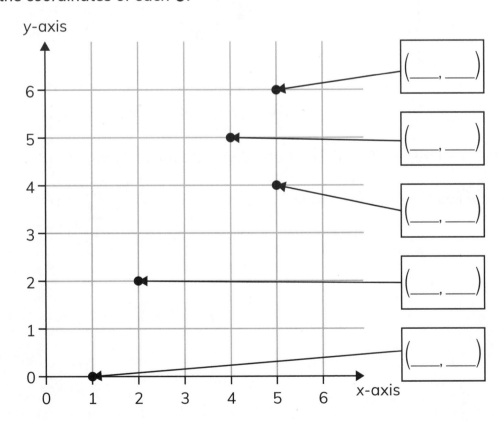

10 Plot these coordinates on the grid.

A (4, 0)

B (0, 1)

C (1, 5)

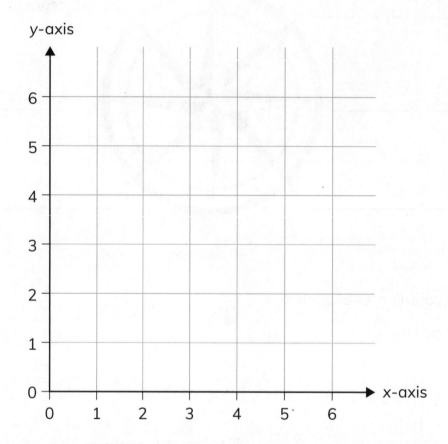

A, B and C are three vertices of a square. Complete the square.

What is the last vertex of the square? _____

> # 18.2 Reflecting 2D shapes

Reflect this shape in the mirror line on the grid.

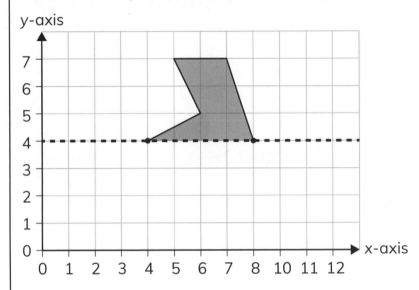

This is a horizontal mirror line.

One edge of the shape is along the mirror line.

The vertices A and E are touching the mirror line. Their reflections will also touch the mirror line.

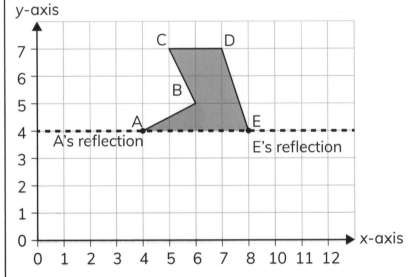

Continued

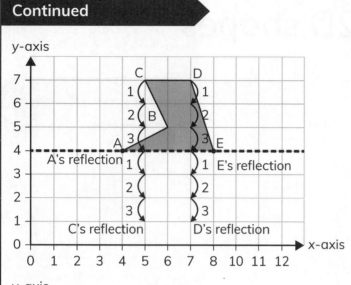

The vertices C and D are both three squares from the mirror line. Their reflections will also be three squares from the mirror line, on the other side of the mirror.

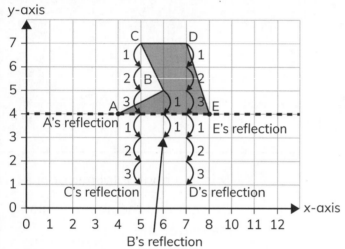

The vertex B is one square from the mirror line. Its reflection will be one square from the mirror line, on the other side of the mirror.

Join the vertices to make the reflection of the whole shape.

Answer:

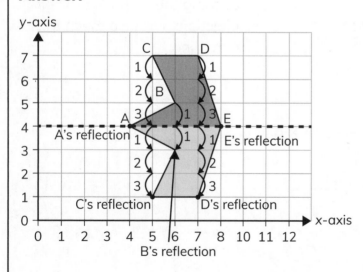

Exercise 18.2

Focus

1   Complete the reflection of these shapes in the mirror line.

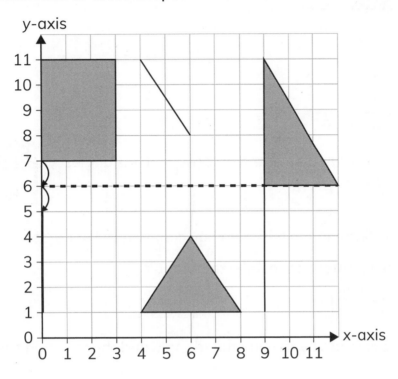

2   Complete the reflection of these shapes in the mirror line.

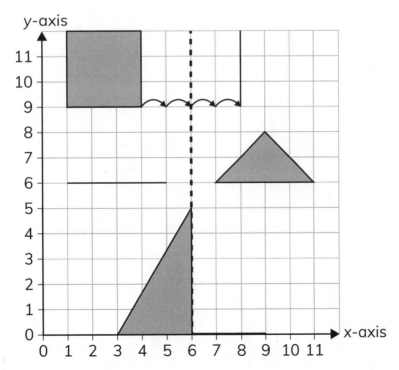

3

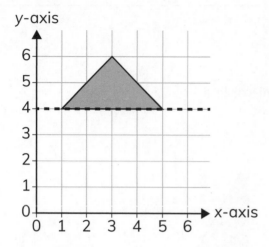

a   What are the coordinates of the vertices of the triangle?

$$\left(\underline{\quad}, \underline{\quad}\right) \qquad \left(\underline{\quad}, \underline{\quad}\right) \qquad \left(\underline{\quad}, \underline{\quad}\right)$$

> **Tip**
>
> Remember ($\leftrightarrow$, $\updownarrow$).

b   Reflect the triangle in the mirror line by counting the squares.

c   Write the coordinates of the reflected triangle.

$$\left(\underline{\quad}, \underline{\quad}\right) \qquad \left(\underline{\quad}, \underline{\quad}\right) \qquad \left(\underline{\quad}, \underline{\quad}\right)$$

d   What shape is made by the original triangle and the reflected triangle together?

_____

Practice

4   Reflect these shapes in the mirror line.

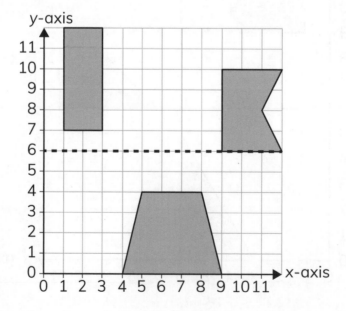

5   Reflect these shapes in the mirror line.

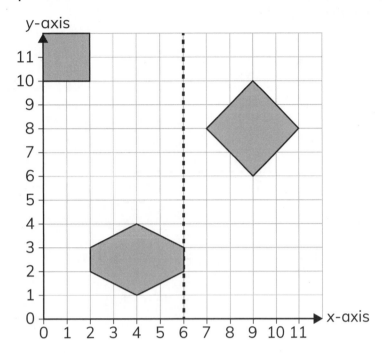

6 **a** List the coordinates of the square on the grid.

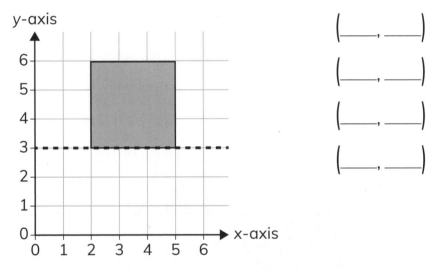

$$\left(\underline{\hphantom{xx}}, \underline{\hphantom{xx}}\right)$$

$$\left(\underline{\hphantom{xx}}, \underline{\hphantom{xx}}\right)$$

$$\left(\underline{\hphantom{xx}}, \underline{\hphantom{xx}}\right)$$

$$\left(\underline{\hphantom{xx}}, \underline{\hphantom{xx}}\right)$$

   b What shape will be made by combining the square with its reflection
in the mirror line?

——————————————

c Draw the reflection of the square in the mirror line to check your answer
to question (b).

7 Draw a rectangle on the grid that will make a square when combined with its reflection in the mirror line.

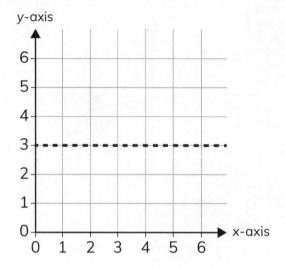

Challenge

8 Reflect these shapes in the mirror line. Count half a square where the edge of the shape is halfway between the grid lines.

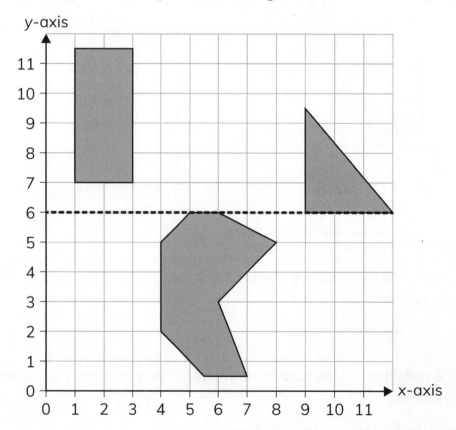

9 Reflect these shapes in the mirror line.

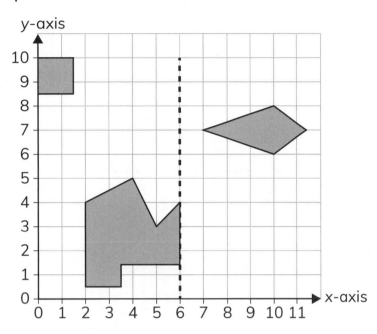

10 Answer questions (a) and (b) before you draw the reflection of the shape.

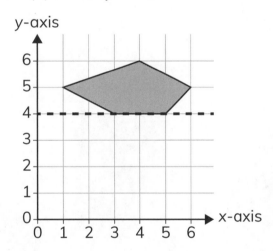

   a What shape will be made by combining this pentagon with its shape reflected in the mirror line?

     _____

   b List the coordinates of the vertices of the reflected shape.

   _____

   c Draw the reflection of the shape on the grid and check your answers for (a) and (b).

11 Draw a pentagon on the grid that will make a hexagon when combined with its reflection in the mirror line.

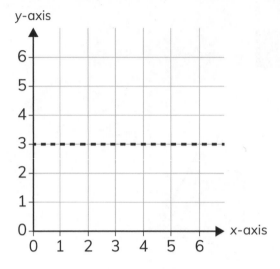